Run in
the Path
of Peace

the Secret of Being Content
No Matter What

MaryEllen Stone

Pat,

I wish many
you many
blessings in
and much in
success in
your writing
Thank you
for your role
in helping me
in this book.

Mary

Run in the Path of Peace—the Secret of Being Content No Matter What is available for purchase at: https://www.createspace.com/3689887

A 25% special discount is available to groups and organizations ordering *Run in the Path of Peace—the Secret of Being Content No Matter What*. Contact MaryEllen at: maryellenstone@hotmail.com for information and the discount code. In the email subject bar enter: book discount request.

Endorsements

"MaryEllen has a bright and engaging writing style that draws readers into the content of *Run in the Path of Peace*."—Sally E. Stuart, Author, *Christian Writers' Market Guide*

"Candidly honest about reactions to life's annoyances and serious traumatic events, MaryEllen Stone skillfully incorporates her professional counseling expertise with her relationship with God and knowledge of Scriptures. The result is a practical resource for developing a lifestyle of peace and contentment. MaryEllen's personal stories demonstrate how a life pattern of sacrificing one's control to the control of our Sovereign God increases freedom and contentment. *Run in the Path of Peace—the Secret of Being Content No Matter What* is definitely a keeper for my library. I look forward to revisiting this book many times."— Linda Potter, Career Member of Wycliffe Bible Translators, having served in Peru, S.A., Papua New Guinea, and the USA

"After my wife passed away, I asked 'Why me?' As I read *Run in the Path of Peace— the Secret of Being Content No Matter What*, I began to understand the abundant life God still has in store for me. This book blessed me and brought me encouragement and His peace. *Run in the Path of Peace* inspires us to look through God's eyes and not our own, for His wonderful blessings are not always wrapped as we expect. Still, they are from His Sovereign hand and bring His plans and purpose to pass."—Lonnie Fuqua, Mechanic

"*Run in the Path of Peace—the Secret of Being Content No Matter What* is so uplifting and challenging I could not wait to return to it each day. In an age when many religious writers spend time and effort describing why the Bible doesn't mean what it says, it is refreshing to read an author who encourages God's people to accept the Word and apply it to their lives. MaryEllen uses captivating anecdotes from her life and from the lives of others to demonstrate how we can integrate Scripture into our circumstances, in good times and in bad. As I read, I found myself applying the book to my life and thinking of people who could benefit from reading it. *Run in the Path of Peace* would be a good study book for personal devotional use, or in a Bible study group."—Shirley Brown, Special Education Teacher

"My mind was challenged from the onset of *Run in the Path of Peace*, to think about and process what I believe the Bible has to say about giving thanks. MaryEllen has done a very good job of articulating her thoughts and reinforcing them with illustrations from the lives of real people, including her own. MaryEllen also gives readers practical ways to apply lessons from the Word in their own lives. I believe a careful study of *Run in the Path of Peace—the Secret of Being Content No Matter What* will benefit anyone who wants to mature in their Christian faith."—Senior Pastor Bob Giles, Faith Family Christian Center

Acknowledgments

To Heather, Claire, Emily, Marcy, Paddy, and Betty, who valiantly shared their testimonies with me and granted permission for their stories to be included in *Run in the Path of Peace—the Secret of Being Content No Matter What*, I give a garland of gratitude. Without their courage and generosity this book would not have been complete.

As well, I offer a bouquet of thanks to members of my writing critique groups for their individual and collective priceless feedback during my writing of *Run in the Path of Peace—the Secret of Being Content No Matter What*—Charolette Conklin, Nancy Laird, Pat Kubin, Margaret Miller, Dan Roberts, and Lori Steed. May the Lord richly bless you all in your writing.

To God, my Lord and Savior, I owe eternal praise and thanksgiving for His love, faithfulness, and guidance.

About the Author

MaryEllen Stone is an inspiring keynote speaker and author, who writes with openness and sincerity seasoned with appropriate humor. She began her career in higher education after earning a Master's Degree in Counseling at the University of Nebraska, Kearney. In 2011, Lower Columbia College in Longview, Washington conferred Faculty Emeritus upon MaryEllen for her thirty years of outstanding and dedicated service. In addition to her career as a college Counselor, MaryEllen practiced as a Licensed Mental Health Counselor for many years. She draws on this knowledge and experience, and her life in Christ to write.

MaryEllen has seen phenomenal life-changing results of freedom, healing, and peace for those who put into practice the principles and techniques shared in *Run in the Path of Peace—the Secret of Being Content No Matter What.*

She and her husband make their home in the Pacific Northwest.

Dear Readers,

Welcome to *Run in the Path of Peace—the Secret of Being Content No Matter What.* In my journey during this writing, I prayed continuously for God's guidance. My mission from the start was threefold: for God to get the glory, for readers to get victory, and for Satan to be defeated. My aim was to hold fast to God's Word throughout the message of this book.

If you come to a section where you wonder how I arrived at that interpretation or conclusion, I ask that you pause and pray for understanding—not only for yourself but for me as well. For if I have misrepresented God's Word in any way, my heartfelt desire is that our Lord will correct me. Above all, I desire to align with His Word and will.

In keeping with proper citations, sidebar and Old Testament quotations refer to LORD (small caps), while New Testament and author references present as Lord.

As God leads, will you pray for the women who have shared their stories in *Run in the Path of Peace?*

I pray for our Lord and Savior's hand upon your life. Even though I may not know you personally, our Heavenly Father does.

Many Blessings in Christ,

Mary

MaryEllen

TABLE OF CONTENTS

❧ ❧

"Give me understanding and I will keep your law and obey it with all my heart. Direct me in the path of your commands, for there I find delight."
Psalm 119:34-35

❧ ❧

PROLOGUE

If early warning signs appeared, we all missed them. Besides, Tara was too happy-go-lucky for anyone to believe anything could be wrong.

When Tara laughed, her shoulders danced with the cadence of her chuckles. Whether at home with family or out with friends, her glee elicited merriment. A devoted mother to a son, age five, and a ten-year-old daughter, Tara loved parenting and looked forward to the future's promise for her and her children.

Tara often called me—after tucking her children in for the night—for long conversations about daily happenings, but mostly to explore the meaning of life and her not-quite-ready-to-accept-Christ-as-her-Savior commitment. At age 39, Tara figured she had lots of time to come to this decision. She figured wrong. Within the year, cancer ravaged her body and stole Tara away from us.

I railed against God. *How could you let this happen? You said we have not because we ask not. I prayed for perfect health for Tara. I asked, believing!*

Days turned into weeks. Still, I shook an emotional fist against the Lord. My insides raw from grief, I felt as if I had been turned inside out—physically, emotionally, and spiritually. Even my professional background did not prepare me for my struggle with this loss. With a Master's Degree in Counseling and a Mental Health License to practice therapy, I have helped others deal with such pain and losses; yet when faced with my own situation, I could not extricate myself from the talons of anger.

Then one day, a thought ticker-taped across my mind: *Give thanks for losing Tara*. Was this the Lord's urging? If so, how could God be so heartless—so cruel—to ask such a ridiculous thing?

The thought persisted, insisted.

All my reasoning and emotions thundered against the demand. An antagonistic part of me reared up and charged. "All right, God. If that's what you want. Thank you for taking Tara's life. Thank you for leaving two children without a parent. Thank you for not answering my prayer." Acid dripped from my words.

Immediately, something came to mind about how God honors obedience. I could hardly see how sarcastically spewing thanks qualified as obedience. However, with lightning clarity in that moment, I realized the urging had not directed me to *be* thankful but to *give* thanks.

I paused to consider the difference. Being thankful would involve emotions—such as joy, happiness, delight. Giving thanks simply required an action, a behavior—uttering the words. But wouldn't it be deceitful to do something I didn't really mean? Still, God was not asking me to *be* thankful. I felt like the epicenter of an emotional tornado. Confusion, anger, and resentment swirled in the tempest. My contrary attitude intensified.

God's presence surrounded me. His love poured over my spirit like warm, soothing oil. Why should He draw close when I willfully pushed away? His presence weakened my dam of sorrow and shame. I began to weep. When finally I could talk, I moaned, "Forgive me."

My healing began—even before learning that Tara had received Christ just before passing away. God had answered my plea for her perfect health, for heaven is the only place where perfect health exists.

This baptismal plunge into a pool of peace amidst a sea of pain proved to be my first step toward contentment no matter what the circumstances. As well, it has paved the path for me to help others find healing and peace within their storms.

Had I known the route God had mapped out for me, I can't say I would have been overly enthusiastic about some of the situations He would give me the opportunity to thank Him for. However, in the pages ahead, you will see why God in His infinite wisdom allows tragedy and pain, and the blessings that breeze our way in the bargain.

I

Are You Sure, Lord?

"I run in the path of your commands, for you have set my
heart free."
Psalm 119:32

The Women's Retreat was just weeks away, and I still didn't have a topic for my keynote speech—at least one the Lord and I could mutually agree upon.

"Seriously, Lord, what do you *really* want me to speak about?" I implored, waiting for an indisputable answer.

I felt His presence. My mind sprouted wings then fluttered to a resistant halt. Although I hadn't heard a voice straight from heaven, I sensed God's urging—the same leading I'd discerned the first time. No way could I deliver *that* message.

"The retreat is supposed to be fun," I protested. What had I gotten myself into? Throughout the next week I put off calling the Conference Coordinator but continued to pray.

The Lord's bidding held fast. Since God obviously wasn't going to change His mind, I guessed I'd better change mine.

I picked up the phone. "Hello, this is MaryEllen, and ... um, I've got the topic for my Keynote Address." I paused, drawing courage.

"Okay," the Coordinator said.

1

More pause. I held my breath, hoping for a last-minute change in orders. "So, what is it?" she asked.

I could no longer put off the inevitable. "Giving thanks for all things." I hurried on to explain, "For example, it's a sunny day and you're on your way to work, when suddenly you realize you have a flat tire. So you thank God not only that it's not raining, but for the flat tire as well."

This time, silence wasn't on my end of the line.

I hastened to fill the dead space between us. "I've been in prayer about it, and every time I sense God giving me the same message." Although the Coordinator, I'm sure, didn't question God's message, I imagined her rifling through an arsenal of Scriptures to head off *my* apparent misunderstanding of the Lord. Leaping ahead of her, I salvoed, "You're probably thinking of the verse in First Thessalonians telling us to give thanks *in* all things." She didn't dispute my mind-reading talents, so I continued. "I already tried that verse-tactic with God." Even now I could fairly see neon arrows shooting from heaven and landing on the word *everything* in my Bible. "Ephesians chapter 5, verse 20 tells us to *always* give thanks for *everything*."

The Coordinator's noiseless distress signals were not unlike the initial frantic scrambling in my own mind when I thought of the anticipated hundred or so Retreat Goers. They would come, I knew, expecting a lighthearted, joyous Saturday of fellowship. Instead, for two hours they would listen to me exhort them—not to thank God *sometimes* for *some* things, but—to thank Him *always* for *everything* as circumstances pertained to them. For the awesome, the annoying, and the awful. For that raise they recently received on their job. For taxes they owed to the IRS. For their kids' chicken pox.

Experiences of death, abuse, financial ruin, and other losses loomed in my mind like a tsunami heading for shore. And that picture only reflected women who obediently took the Scripture to heart. What about the more-than-likely volcanic eruption of bitterness and anger at the mere thought of thanking God for atrocities endured?

Or what if, after my presentation, silence ushered me off the stage and out the door? What if these women wouldn't or couldn't share deep, personal situations with someone they'd never met before? What if, after encouraged to give thanks for the bad and the ugly, animosity simmered beneath the surface? Would they leave the retreat wounded? How could I possibly avoid a disaster?

"Oh, there's one more thing," I said to the Coordinator. "When you print the flyers, list my Keynote Address as 'Running in the Path of His Commands.'"

I could almost hear her mental wheels whirring: *Yeah sure, get 'em there with an optimistic title, then ambush 'em at the pass.* Thankfully, she kept this to herself, agreed to my request, politely hung up, and left me to my formidable task.

How could I effectively convey the healing and peace I'd experienced in thanking God for the loss of my friend? However painful losing a friend, it still is not the same as watching a parent, sibling, spouse—or child—die. Certainly, the church would brim with women who had suffered such devastating losses.

Since I believed it was God's idea for me to encourage these women to thank Him for all things, I would rely upon Him to deliver the goods. I turned to the Bible and identified with Paul who wrote: "It is true that I am an ordinary, weak human being, but I don't use human plans and methods to win my battles. I use God's mighty weapons ... to knock down the devil's strongholds ... break down every proud argument against God and every wall that can be built to keep men from finding him ... and change them into men whose hearts' desire is obedience to Christ." (2 Cor. 10:3-5 *The Living Bible*)

Rolling up my spiritual sleeves, I delved into God's ammunition depot, arming myself against anticipated defenses. Like constructing a house, I had to first build a foundation—one based upon God's wisdom, not on my own understanding. If I could help the women see things through His eyes, then they would be prepared to do as He asks—to give thanks for *all* things.

Scripture verses fell into place. Finally, I was ready.

Retreat Day Arrives

I step through the old country church door, draw a deep breath, and utter a prayer. I receive a warm welcome by acquaintances, new and old.

Soon, I gird myself with the music team's introductory praise and worship. I sense God's presence. Armed with His Word, I advance to the podium and ask, "If someone offered you a gift that is perfect, trustworthy, right, radiant, pure, sure, righteous, precious, and sweet, would you jump at the chance to receive it? Especially when you learn this gift will revive your soul, make you wise, give you joy, improve your sight, provide warning, and offer great reward?"

My eyes scan a multitude of eager faces ready to accept such a present. The women sit attentively. *Thank you, Lord, that you want to bless these ladies.* I relax, feeling confident that the groundwork God has helped me prepare will sustain the building yet to come. I launch into the basic tenets of "Running in the Path of His Commands."

Throughout the morning, I lay the foundation, raise the framework. Ladies take copious notes. They smile with expectant joyous faces as we dismiss for lunch, an upbeat affair, peppered with laughter and seasoned with camaraderie. Mealtime passes quickly, and we return to the sanctuary and resume with singing. Praise and worship cement my trust in the Lord's leading and faithfulness.

Once again at the podium, I usher the women into Ephesians 5:20. I read from the *The New International Version Study Bible*, starting in the middle of the nineteenth verse, "Sing and make music in your heart to the Lord, always giving thanks to God the Father for everything, in the name of our Lord Jesus Christ."

I notice many reread the verse. *Are they comprehending "for everything"?*

I sense skepticism, hesitation. I forge ahead, connecting "Running in the Path of His Commands" to giving thanks for all things.

As I invite the women to draw from their morning's assignment—to write down their physical, emotional, and spiritual wounds—and to thank God silently for each item on their list, I remind them that He does not ask us to *be* thankful, but to simply thank Him for allowing it to happen.

Now it is time to break into small groups for prayer and support. I encourage them to share whatever they wish to disclose with their group. Initially, barely audible sighs float through the air. Then, voices stutter-start, slicing through the thick fabric of heaviness. More voices join the process. Tears streak down cheeks. Prayers. Hugs. Audible "Thank you's." If I could see spiritually, no doubt I would witness shackles falling away. A sense of freedom fills the room.

At one table, I am drawn in by a woman who says, "When you asked us to give thanks for *all* things, I didn't see how it could be appropriate to give thanks for the effect my husband's prior involvement in pornography has on our marriage. But in doing so, I was able to minister and give encouragement to a sister in Christ who suffers the same experience with her husband."

What a perfect example of Ephesians 5:15, "making the most of every opportunity, because the days are evil."

In another group … "My husband passed away two years ago. I know he is in heaven." Sobbing. "I am not thankful he is gone but when I gave thanks for his passing, I felt a release. Now, I think I can move on with my life." And so the comments go. I leave the retreat marveling at God's love and pathway to healing and release.

Post-Retreat

Although I left the retreat exhilarated, it wasn't long before thoughts nagged at me. Had everyone truly been able to thank God for everything? Even though all women had appeared to embrace Ephesians 5:20, what if some had closed their eyes in disbelief, resistance, or worse yet, in agony over tragedies in their lives?

While still on earth, I will never know the answers to these questions. But this I do know: The seed was planted, and God will bring into fruition that which is sown.

A few weeks following the retreat, a woman approached me in the grocery store. She said, "I was molested as a child. I've spent years in therapy. Nothing worked—until you asked us to thank God for everything. It didn't make sense. I didn't want to. But I did it. You can't imagine the healing I've experienced! For the first time since childhood, I'm not tormented."

How could I have ever doubted His direction for the retreat? The Lord had faithfully ministered to those who had suffered abuse, lost a child to death, put up with the pain of a

> *"Pain-induced tears cleanse my eyes so that I may see the sight and might of my Lord and Savior."*—MaryEllen

husband's infidelity, endured depression, and so on. He led them from Retreat Victims to Retreat Victors. God's Word had prepared them to take the step of faith and thank Him for these things—if not in that country church that Saturday, then at a time when they are ready.

Where Are You Along Your Path?

- Do you feel defeated by daily bills, overwhelmed by never-ending chores, or rubbed raw by sandpaper relationships?

- Are you living in the present pain of past hurts?
- Do you want to forgive but can't step into the freedom of forgiveness?
- Do you struggle with "Letting go and letting God"—unable to relinquish control and accept *what is*?
- Are you in the midst of a tragedy or current crisis?

In other words, are you experiencing emotional stress or distress? Or undergoing ongoing or temporary spiritual duress?

I invite you to discover the scriptural foundation the Lord laid for the women at the retreat, and the healing and peace God has in store especially for you as you continue to read. I pray you experience the truth of this message in your step to embrace Ephesians 5:20—always giving God thanks for all things. May you be freed once and for all from that which holds you emotionally hostage.

∽

As you pray today, I encourage you to make the following prayer your own.

Invitation to Personal Prayer

Lord, please help me understand that giving thanks for all things will
bring rewards. Thank you for your faithfulness. Amen.

Memory Verse

"I run in the path of your commands, for you have set my heart free."
Psalm 119:32

~ 2 ~

When God's Entreaties Don't Make Sense

"Trust in the LORD with all your heart and lean not unto
your own understanding; in all your ways acknowledge him,
and he will make your paths straight."
Proverbs 3:5-6

Upon sharing Ephesians 5:20—God's entreaty for us to thank Him for all things—I am frequently met with skepticism and questions. And rightly so, for this is a verse that simply doesn't make sense in our temporal way of thinking. I am thankful for these challenges, for they have caused me to delve deeply into the Bible, not only to add to my limited understanding but to attempt to see this verse through God's perspective.

Perhaps these same questions have cropped up in your mind.

Q: You emphasize that God doesn't command us to be thankful but to give thanks. Doesn't this contradict other verses where we are urged to be thankful?

A: The Bible is filled with verses where we are commissioned to be thankful—the last portion of Colossians 3:15, for example, clearly states, "... And be thankful." In verses such as this, God sets an overarching spiritual standard.

Certainly, we must not dismiss God's calling for us to be thankful, but at the same time, we need to acknowledge His distinction between *being thankful* in our spirit and *giving thanks* for everything. Nowhere in His Word does God exhort us to *be thankful* for all things.

Q: Still, aren't you taking Ephesians 5:20 out of context? Don't we have to consider the whole Bible?

A: Context is critical, and we certainly must consider the entire Bible. Ephesians 5:20 is supported by a multitude of Scriptures—from the Old and New Testaments alike—many of which I integrate into the text of this book. I invite you to meditate on each passage and pray for insight and wisdom as you unearth the truth of God's Word. You may want to start a notebook or journal in which you keep a record of these Bible verses so you can return to them for further study. At the end of this book, you will find how all of these verses come together to form a path.

Q: Perhaps something is lost in the translation from the original Greek manuscripts. Shouldn't you question the translation's correct meaning and implication?

A: Not all of us are schooled in Greek, Hebrew, or Aramaic languages. Therefore, we have only the Bibles God has provided us. Throughout this text, I have used the *New International Version*, except where otherwise noted. Following is Ephesians 5:20 from five other versions as taken from *The New Testament in Four Versions*, Christianity Today Edition.

> *King James Version:* "Giving thanks always for all things unto God and the Father in the name of our Lord Jesus Christ." (602).[1]

> *Revised Standard Version:* "always and for everything giving thanks in the name of our Lord Jesus Christ to God the Father" (602).

> *Phillips Modern English:* "Thank God at all times for everything in the name of our Lord Jesus Christ" (603).

---

1 Christianity Today Edition. *The New Testament in Four Versions.* (New York: The Iverson-Ford Associates, 1963), 602-603.

The New English Bible: "and in the name of our Lord Jesus Christ give thanks every day for everything to our God and Father" (603).

Each of the above translations has similar if not exact presentations of Ephesians 5:20. These renditions come from scholars who studied original Greek texts for clarity, accuracy, and literary quality. They labored over lexical, grammatical, and semantic details and were faithful to the syntax of language and the contextual meaning of words. Because of this, I have confidence that the Lord helped them preserve the truth of His Word.

Q: Yet, your theology seems a bit off-kilter. Aren't you taking the Bible too literally?

A: If I start changing words such as *all* to *some* or *always* to *sometimes*, I put myself in the position of deciding what should and what shouldn't be. For example, what a shaky foundation I would have with the following exchanges: (italics mine)

"Jesus replied: 'Love the Lord your God with *some of* your heart and with *part of* your soul and with *portions of* your mind.'" (Matt. 22:37)

"But when he, the Spirit of truth, comes, he will guide you into *some* truth …." (Jn. 16:13)

"Through him *some* who believe *are* justified from *some things* you could not be justified from by the law of Moses." (Acts 13:39)

"Since we have these promises, dear friends, let us purify ourselves from *some things* that contaminate body and spirit, perfecting holiness out of reverence for God." (2 Cor. 7:1)

In Mark chapter 9, verse 23, Jesus tells us: "Everything is possible for him who believes." Is the emphasis here on *everything* or *belief*? Perhaps both. Isn't Jesus encouraging us to not put limits on what God can do? Why, then, is it in our human nature to argue that Ephesians 5:20 doesn't really mean we should thank Him for *everything*? Shouldn't we trust in Him? When we doubt that everything really means *every thing*, we fail to accept His power to help us grow into the likeness of Christ, who came to earth and walked among us to teach us so that we might mature in the knowledge of our Creator. He did not want us to remain as babies, helpless in the storms of life.

When we refuse to believe He literally means *everything* in Ephesians 5:20, it is possible we have hardened our hearts, holding fast to a theological interpretation

9

that is comfortable for us. In my initial grappling with this verse, I teetered on the brink of futility regarding my own thinking. It was only at the moment of "leaning not unto my own understanding but in all my ways acknowledging Him" that I experienced His understanding about giving thanks for my friend's death. Put another way: Only when I gave up trying to fit Ephesians into the construct of my thinking and gave thanks, did I come into alignment with His perspective.

Thanksgiving truly is an antidote to hardening of the heart.

Thanksgiving is also like a door handle. Seizing it allows us to gain a personal grasp on the Word of God in all its power. Incredible things happen when we're open to the possibilities in His Word.

Q: So, *all* things means we should thank God for terrorism and all the evils in the world, right?

A: Again, context is critical. The beginning of the paragraph reads, "Be very careful, then, how you live—not as unwise but as wise, making the most of every opportunity, because the days are evil." (Eph. 5:15-16) The message is clearly directed to each of us individually. Therefore, the instruction to thank God for all things refers to things as they affect *you*. So, yes, if you are the object of a terrorist attack, then God has a plan to bless you in this situation, and thanking Him for allowing it will help you come to this realization, to see His perspective on the whole thing. This is an extremely difficult concept to embrace, but as you read through the rest of *Run in the Path of Peace* you will see how "in all things God works for the good of those who love him, who have been called according to his purpose." (Rom. 8:28)

Q: Okay, if everything means every thing, wouldn't that include sins I commit?

A: This argument is like that in Romans 6: "What shall we say, then? Shall we go on sinning so that grace may increase? By no means!" God calls us to repentance for the sins we have committed. His Word does not, nor ever will, contradict itself. Therefore, I cannot give thanks for my willful disobedience. I cannot say, "Thank you, God, that I steal things." For " … the sinful mind is hostile to God. It does not submit to God's law, nor can it do so." (Rom. 8:7)

Peter sums this up in 1 Peter 4:15: "If you suffer, it should not be as a murderer or thief or any other kind of criminal, or even as a meddler."

So, while we are to give thanks for all things we endure, we cannot give thanks for our own willful sins. To do so would deny and contradict everything for which Christ died. That's the good news … when we repent of our sins, and ask forgiveness for them, we are cleansed from them.

Q: You are saying "don't thank God for my sins but give thanks for sins others perpetrate against me". This sounds contradictory.

A: I am responsible for my own actions, accountable to God for what I do. Jesus made this clear at the end of the twenty-first chapter of John when He told Peter to follow Him. Peter looked at another disciple and asked, "… what about him?" Jesus answered that was between Him and the other disciple. In other words, don't concern yourself with someone else; "You must follow me." We cannot control others; we only have control over our own actions. Besides, God assures us that even when others harm us, in *all* things He works for the good of those who love Him. (Rom. 8:28) This is truly something deserving our thanks.

Thus, God directs us to thank Him not for others' sins but for all things as they affect us. He essentially calls us to trust that He is greater than others' sins. He can use sinful acts against us to help us grow in our faith and mature into Christ-likeness—just as He used Jesus' crucifixion as an atonement for our sins.

An acquaintance recently said to me, "My father died when I was only eight years old. I would never, ever thank God for Daddy's death because death is of sin." He then went into a discourse saying had man not sinned in the Garden of Eden, mankind would not now face death.

As for death, I thank God for Jesus' death because without it my sins would never have been covered by His blood.

While it isn't stated outright, it would seem Jesus' attitude regarding the evil done to Him was one of thanksgiving to God for having the opportunity to bear witness to us. In fact, in another garden—the Garden of Gethsemane—praying prior to His arrest and imminent crucifixion, Jesus petitioned God to bless his followers with the full measure of the *joy* He had within Him (Jn. 17:13). Even though He was overwhelmed to the point of death (Matt. 26:38), Jesus never let go of His joy.

11

Peter makes the connection between Christ's attitude towards suffering and ours: "Therefore, since Christ suffered in his body, arm yourselves also with the same attitude, because he who has suffered in his body is done with sin." (I Pet. 4:1) "... do not be surprised at the painful trial you are suffering, as though something strange were happening to you. But rejoice that you participate in the sufferings of Christ, so that you may be overjoyed when his glory is revealed." (I Pet. 4:12-13)

> *"I am not about convincing you of theology, but am convinced that if you thank God for all things, regardless of how sound it sounds, you will experience healing and freedom."—MaryEllen*

Thus Peter tells us that by rejoicing, even in the face of suffering at the hands of others' sin, we can overcome sin. This means victory for us.

And peace!

Joseph is a perfect example of this principle. His brothers sold him into slavery then lied about it to their father, saying a wild animal had killed Joseph. To prove their lie, they even went so far as to bloody the beautiful coat of many colors their father had given Joseph. Sins against Joseph didn't end there. Even though he did what was right in the sight of God, Joseph was falsely accused of things that landed him in prison. In the end, God used Joseph to deliver the nation of Israel! As Joseph said to his brothers, "You intended to harm me, but God intended it for good to accomplish what is now being done, the saving of many lives." (Gen. 50:20)

The key here is to rightfully distinguish between others' sins and others' sins against us. To align with God's Word, it is important to thank Him for the latter, for that is where we can put our faith and trust in our Creator who can use harm done to us to accomplish great things. Joseph's life is but one example. In the chapters ahead, you will read of contemporary women whose lives also illustrate this point.

Q: It seems as if you're saying thanking God for bad things makes everything all right. Isn't taking one verse, i.e. Ephesians 5:20, too simplistic?

A: Yes, it is simplistic in that uttering a few words is all God asks us to do in Ephesians 5:20. However, His promise is not that our obedience will make everything all right—on the outside—but that it will unite us with Him, in essence, shepherd us into internal peace. It is a simple command that simply works.

"God's promises work their wonders while we see and act on external realities and refuse to be affected by temporal things to the contrary."—F.F. Bosworth

My husband and I were sitting on our deck reading the newspaper as evening approached. Mosquitoes descended upon us. Noticing my husband's aggravation, I asked, "Did you know words can come against those pests and keep them from bothering you?"

His look said, "Yeah, right."

I folded my word-filled paper into a swat weapon and offered it to him.

He took it and moments later conceded, "It works."

The same principle pertains to Scripture verses. When we grasp hold of God's Word to counter assaults against us, the perpetrator or situation can no longer "sting" us.

Paul captures this truth in describing the weapons available to us. "The weapons we fight with are not the weapons of the world. On the contrary, they have divine power to demolish strongholds. We demolish arguments and every pretension that sets itself up against the knowledge of God, and we take every thought captive to make it obedient to Christ." (2 Cor. 10:4-5) Again in Ephesians 6:16-17, Paul encourages us to put on the armor of God by seizing the shield of faith and the sword of the Spirit, which is the Word of God. When we thank God for all things, we brandish this sword and tear a hole in the darkness of bad things, allowing God's light to permeate our souls.

In short, the simple things of God work—and confound the wise.

Q: It is one thing to thank God for annoyances but another entirely to give Him thanks for tragedies which catapult us into pain and suffering. Should we simply bypass the grieving process when we encounter loss?

A: Not at all. Grief is a God-given emotion that helps us work through death and other losses. Wailing and mourning are essential in the healing process. Thanking God for the loss actually assists us in moving through the steps of grief.

Q: Does the verse "all things work to the good" include everyone?

A: It includes all God's children who love Him and who have been called to His purpose. (Romans 8:28)

Q: Isn't everyone a child of God? And if not, why wouldn't He extend this covering to everyone?

A: God wants to welcome everyone into His fold. But it is up to the individual whether or not (s)he wants to join His family.

"God has a door open and waiting for you to step through—a door of opportunity called Thanksgiving. You can wait until your circumstances merit thanks, or you can thank Him now for the hardship or pain. If you choose the latter, be prepared for your chains to fall away—not chains of circumstance, but internal chains of bitterness, anger, or heartache."—MaryEllen

Let's use the example of a father, Dave, who has a health insurance policy on his children, Tawna, Josiah, and Max. Obviously, the policy doesn't promise they won't get sick or have accidents, but it does assure them that if they do, they are covered—they can get the help they need to heal. Along comes Serena, who asks to be put on the policy. The problem is, she isn't Dave's child. So, she can't tap into the coverage, not unless she asks Dave to adopt her and he agrees.

Q: How do I become a child of God?

A: By telling Him (and meaning it, of course) that you want to accept Jesus into your life and that you truly want Christ to be the Lord of your life.

Ask Him to forgive your sins. Admit that you no longer want to do things your way, but His way. It's as simple as that. God is waiting for you to give your heart to Him—waiting and willing to bless you.

Q: What if I am a brand new baby in Christ and don't understand all the concepts within these pages?

A: Trust comes by taking the first step. If you acknowledge Him in everything you do and don't try to have everything make sense, He will make your paths straight, just as He promises in Proverbs 3:5-6. Even though you may not see things clearly now, the Lord promises, "I will lead the blind by ways they have not known, along unfamiliar paths I will guide them; I will turn the darkness into light before them and make the rough places smooth. These things I will do; I will not forsake them." (Isaiah 42:16)

"Understanding is the reward of faith. Therefore seek not understanding that thou mayest believe, but believe that thou mayest understand."—Augustine (c. 416)

Perhaps you have other questions or concerns I haven't covered regarding "When God's Entreaties Don't Make Sense". I urge you to take these to God in prayer. Beyond that, I encourage you to consider the accounts of Biblical men in the following chapter who didn't try to make sense of God's commands but simply obeyed.

༒

Invitation to Personal Reflection

List your questions and/or concerns regarding Ephesians 5:20—to thank Him for all things. I encourage you to place them before God, trusting Him for guidance and His perspective.

1. _____
_____

2. _____
_____

3. _____
_____

4. _____
_____

5. _____
_____

Invitation to Personal Prayer

- **If you do not yet know Christ as your Savior:**

God, please reveal yourself to me. I want to know you and what you have for me. Please come into my life. Even though I don't yet know all it entails, I ask Jesus to be Lord of my life. Please forgive me for my past wrongdoings. Thank you for receiving me now as a child of God. Amen.

- **If you are a brand new Christian:**

Lord, I'm not sure I am ready to thank you for tragedies in my life. This picks open emotional pain. At the same time, I want to trust you. Please lead me through the steps toward total trust in you. I put my hand—trembling as it is—in yours. Amen.

- **If you are a seasoned child of God:**

Jesus, I trust you have only good in store for me. I realize this doesn't mean everything in my life will go smoothly—at least on the outside. But I trust you are leading me toward an even greater inner peace. Hallelujah for your faithfulness. I eagerly await this next step of my journey in Christ. Amen.

Memory Verse

"Open my eyes that I may see wonderful things in your law."
Psalm 119:18

∾ 3 ∾

Role Models of Obedience

"Now faith is being sure of what we hope for and certain
of what we do not see. This is what the ancients
were commended for."
Hebrews 11:1-2

Throughout history, God has proven His ways are not our ways. Time and again, He directed characters of the Bible to do things completely out of the realm of sound reasoning—at least in the sense of human logic. Let's consider a few instances:

- **God directed Noah …**
… to build an ark in preparation for a forthcoming flood that was to wipe out all people on the earth except Noah and his family. If that weren't enough for Noah to wrap his mind around, how do you suppose he came to terms with the next part of God's command? I imagine it sounding something like this, "Oh, and by the way, Noah, the ark needs to be big enough to carry seven of every kind of clean animals—males and their mates; two of every unclean creatures, males and mates; and seven of every kind of birds, males and mates; and every kind of food to be eaten to keep the animals and fowls alive."

So, here you have a man 500-plus years old, consigned to manual labor of Titanic magnitude, building how big a boat? However, that may have been the easy part. Perhaps Noah's greatest challenge came when he shared all this with his wife.

"You're gonna do what, Noah?"

I don't know about you, but if my husband came to me with this kind of information, I'd be on the phone making an appointment for his mental health assessment. On the other hand, maybe Noah's wife, who bore their three sons when Noah was 500 years old, took it all in stride—as if it were nothing out of the ordinary. Even at that, how must Noah's wife have felt about losing friends who would perish?

> *"Obedience even in the face of nothing that makes sense is demonstration of trust and faith in God."—MaryEllen*

At any rate, Noah set about gathering materials and building the ark, most likely in the face of jeering neighbors. Resolute, he persevered throughout the many years it took to complete this task. I would have loved to see the incredulous look on his neighbors' faces when giraffes, ants, elephants, mice, aardvarks, ostriches, hummingbirds, and the rest showed up. That would have to be one of the best examples in the history of the world of belief vs. disbelief.

- **God gave Abraham …**

… a child to his previously barren ninety-something-year-old wife, then told Abraham to sacrifice his son Isaac. Whoa! Where's the sense in that? Or at least a logic we in our finite thinking can imagine?

I have serious doubts Abraham shared this with Sarah, at least beforehand, since she had the propensity to make things difficult for him. For example, earlier, Sarah—unable to bear children—suggested that Abraham sleep with her maidservant Hagar so Abraham could sire a child. Later Sarah went to Abraham and complained, "You are responsible for the wrong I am suffering. I put my servant in your arms, and now that she knows she is pregnant, she despises me." (Gen. 16:5) Caught in the middle, Abraham told her to do as she wished with Hagar. Consequently, Sarah mistreated her. Still later, Sarah overheard the Lord telling Abraham that she would bear him a son. Sarah laughed and doubted. Immediately, God asked Abraham why Sarah laughed and questioned that she would have a child. At this, Sarah lied, asserting she did not laugh.

Given this side of Sarah, if you were Abraham, would you have told her, "Incidentally, Hon, I'm taking our son Isaac to the mountain to kill him as a sacrifice to God."? Indeed, having to contend with Sarah adds an even greater dimension of "non-sense" for Abraham to carry out God's request. Still, Abraham did not question the Lord in this. In following through with the Lord's entreaty to lay Isaac on the altar as a sacrifice, Abraham proved his trust and faith in God. How relieved Abraham must have been when God honored this by sparing Isaac's life!

- **God encouraged Moses …**

… to lead the Israelites out of Egypt, not by way of a road that was a shorter route, but around a desert and toward the Red Sea. With the Egyptian army in pursuit, this would certainly hem in the fleeing Israelites. As the enemy approached, the Israelites were terrified and cried out to Moses. Moses then cried out to the Lord. At this point God told Moses, "Raise your staff and stretch out your hand over the sea to divide the water so that the Israelites can go through the sea on dry ground." (Ex. 14:16)

Here was Moses with a terrified, shrieking, chaotic mass of people on one side and charging horsemen and chariots on the other. And all he had to do was lift his staff and stretch out his hand?

I've heard it said the Red Sea was low at that season. I've read other accounts that put it at high tide. Either way—mud or deep water—would prevent a whole nation of people crossing before a hot-on-their-trail army overtook them.

Yet God's instructions were clear. Didn't make sense, but nonetheless clear. Holding tight to his staff and trusting God, Moses lifted it heavenward over the waters. God parted the waters and held them at bay until the last of the Israelites were across. At that moment, the sea folded, swallowing the enemy.

- **God directed Joshua …**

… to bring down the walls of Jericho with a shout. Well, actually it wasn't as simple as that. First Joshua was to "March around the city once with all the armed men." (Josh. 6:3) They were to do this for six days. At the same time, priests were to carry trumpets of rams' horns in front of the ark. On the seventh day, they were to march around Jericho seven times while the priest blew the trumpets. At the long trumpet blast, all the people were to shout.

Voilà! The walls collapsed, and God gave Joshua and his army the city and all that was in it, to be devoted to the Lord.

Who'd have ever thought a city could be seized with a shout?

- **God instructed Gideon ...**

... who faced enemy troops as thick as locusts, to send some of his army of 32,000 home because he had too many soldiers. What, 32,000 against a virtually uncountable number? In fact, the enemy's "camels could no more be counted than the sand on the seashore." (Jdg. 6:12) Gideon obeyed, leaving him with 10,000 men. If I were Gideon, I would've been sweating bullets. Okay, so they didn't have bullets back then. But wait; this wasn't the last of it. God then informed Gideon he still had too many in his army. Long story short, Gideon was left with a battalion of only 300 men.

Just when you think it couldn't get any stranger, it did. In addition to the trumpets and a shout with which God had armed Joshua's troops, the Lord mixed it up a bit by adding jars to Gideon's arsenal. Following God's instructions, when Gideon and his small army reached the edge of the enemy's camp, they blew their trumpets, broke the jars in their hands, and shouted, "A sword for the LORD and for Gideon." (Judges 7:20)

Sure doesn't make sense to me, but it worked. God caused the enemy soldiers to turn on each other with their swords. Thus Gideon and his small band of 300 won the battle!

God in His infinite wisdom has a plan for all of us to win our battles—even if the plan doesn't make sense to us. In each of the instances above, as Noah, Abraham, Moses, Joshua, and Gideon obeyed out of trust, God

> *"Gideon's lamps were revealed when his soldiers' pitchers were broken. If our pitchers are broken for the LORD and His gospels' sake, lamps will be revealed that otherwise would have stayed hidden and unseen ... Out of affliction's dark comes spiritual light."—John Bunyon*

responded with blessings. Today, when we obey His commands, we have blessings awaiting as well.

- **Jesus invites Peter …**

… to "Come." It was night and a storm tossed the disciples around in a small boat in the middle of a lake. They looked up, terrified when they saw someone approaching, walking on the water. Even after Jesus identified himself and told them not to be afraid, Peter wanted confirmation.

"'Lord, if it's you,' Peter replied, 'tell me to come to you on the water.'"

'Come,' Jesus said. Then Peter got down out of the boat, walked on the water and came toward Jesus. But when he saw the wind, he was afraid and, beginning to sink, cried out 'Lord, save me!' Immediately Jesus reached out his hand and caught him. 'You of little faith,' he said, 'why did you doubt?'" (Matt. 14:29-31)

Although Peter's walk on water is a perfect example of a person being sunk by doubt, it is an even more astounding example of obedient response as proof of being buoyed by trust. It is only when we take our eyes off Jesus and let our surroundings assault us that we break the sustaining connection with Christ. When we thank Him for our circumstances, our eyes are on our Lord and Savior, not on our situation.

God is calling to you to "Come," to put your faith in Him, to place your hand in His, to let Him guide you through the tempests of life. There is no storm greater than His power to keep you afloat. By responding to His commands—even when they don't make sense—you will have peace that passes all understanding and receive blessings beyond measure.

A question you may have, however, is "How can I know it is the Lord leading me?" This is why it is crucial for you to be steeped in God's Word. He will never contradict Himself, nor will He lead you to do something contrary to His laws. Knowing the Bible and experiencing intimacy with Christ through prayer provides you with a compass. If you doubt you are receiving divine direction, it is better to take time to pray about it than to act immediately. God knows our hearts and will honor our desire to make sure it is He who is leading. Generally, if you feel an urgency to act, it may be your own desires or the enemy—Satan—who wants to mislead you.

As you spend time pondering on the Biblical examples in this chapter, I encourage you to record your insights as well as make the prayer your own.

〰

Invitation to Personal Reflection

These Biblical examples have helped me:

Invitation to Personal Prayer

Lord Jesus, I want to be obedient to you, which is why I want to know
your voice. Please help me store your Word in my heart and mind.
Please check my spirit when I am prompted by my erroneous thinking
or by the enemy. Thank you.

Memory Verse
---

*"All Scripture is God-breathed and is useful for teaching, rebuking, correcting
and training in righteousness, so that the man of God may be thoroughly
equipped for every good work."*
2 Timothy 3:16-17

4

God's Commands, The Way to Go

"Direct me in the path of your commands, for there
I find delight."
Psalm 119:32

God's commands. Do you consider them demanding, rigid, or burdensome? If so, it would seem our Lord is a hard taskmaster.

Our Heavenly Father views His commands differently. In His eyes, "The Law of the LORD is perfect, reviving the soul. The statutes of the LORD are trustworthy, making wise the simple. The precepts of the LORD are right, giving joy to the heart. The commands of the LORD are radiant, giving light to the eyes. The fear of the LORD is pure, enduring forever. The ordinances of the LORD are sure and altogether righteous. They are more precious than gold, than much pure gold; they are sweeter than honey, than honey from the comb. By them is your servant warned; in keeping them there is great reward." (Ps. 19:7-11)

When I was a baby Christian and before I delved into the Word of God, I considered His commands to be confining. Then one day I noticed our kitten, Smokey, engaged in a fencing duel, pawing and pouncing against the pampas grass' parries and thrusts. Suddenly, a gust of wind joined the fun, lifting one of the plant's long, slender blades toward fencing of another kind. My attention turned to the strings of barbed wire that enclosed our green pasture.

I thought of dangers lurking beyond the fence: Our son-in-law spotted a cougar within a mile of our home. The local newspaper reported escaped hybrid wolves in our area. Deep canyons pose peril just a stone's throw from the edge of our property. The surrounding dense forest, where high winds tumble towering trees, offers little shelter from storms. Impenetrable blackberry brambles grab and tear and refuse to relinquish their jurisdiction. All these threaten safety. Granted, the five-foot-high fence won't keep predators from crossing over—as evidenced by the black bear that lumbered onto our property last summer—but the odds of our livestock being attacked is certainly lessened if the cattle stay within the barbed borders.

While pondering this, a message seeped into my thoughts: *God's Word is like that fence—protection so I will not stray into danger.*

My mind somersaulted back to instances when I rebelled against His fences: a joy ride of excitement down a country road; the enticing greener grass of dating an older, much more "experienced" man when I was in my teens; the lure of an alcohol-induced state of consciousness … the list went on. Then my thoughts cartwheeled to the consequences of those wanderings: my car in the ditch; the heartache of an unhealthy relationship; and the regret and embarrassment of my drunken behavior.

> *"But from everlasting to everlasting the* LORD's *love is with those who fear him and his righteousness with their children's children—with those who keep his covenant and remember to obey his precepts."—Psalm 103:17-18*

When my behavior wasn't corralled, God's Word seemed harsh and confining rather than loving and protective. No wonder Jesus is called the Good Shepherd. Just as we have a fence securing our cattle, likewise He offers safeguards to His flock through His statutes. And just as the enclosure we have for our animals didn't keep our Nellie from breaking through one day in May, and running into the wilderness to never return, so God's commands don't stop all tragedies from coming into our lives. But the likelihood of bad things happening to us is diminished the more we stay within His law.

This is so because His laws are perfect, trustworthy, wise, and right. They bring joy to our hearts and help us see clearly. Indeed, they are precious and sweet. (Ps. 19:7-11)

As this truth about His "fences" became real for me, and maybe because my husband used to be a heavy equipment operator, I envisioned God's commands like a road dozer forging ahead in my behalf, clearing debris that would otherwise come crashing down upon me. For example, His law against gossiping works to head problems off at the pass, i.e. to help us avoid the fallout of our careless words.

Ever present, the Command Dozer forges a trail for us to follow. "Let the word of Christ dwell in you …" (Col. 3:16). This entreaty levels the road in front of us—as promised in Isaiah 42:16. In other words, He will make the rough places smooth—filling sinkholes we are prone to fall into, such as the habit of not taking time to read the Bible. By hiding His Word in our heart, we can avoid pits along our paths—situations such as dishonest gain, sexual immorality—that would cause us to stumble and get off track.

Are you ever weighed down by despair and simply can't get beyond it? The Command Dozer pushes aside this obstacle by the power of the Word: "Through Jesus, therefore, let us continually offer to God a sacrifice of praise …." (Heb. 13:15) How does this work? Isaiah 61:3 reveals that a garment of praise replaces a spirit of despair.

Whereas the Command Dozer initially provided a visual concept revealing the almighty power of His Word, the more I pondered God's commands, the more I came back to Psalm 119:105: "Your Word is a lamp to my feet and a light for my path." A mental image appeared of a lamp in my hand, albeit a contemporary one much like the Light Saber which delights my five-year-old grandson. I call this Almighty Beam the Command Illuminator.

God was taking me to the next level of understanding. The Command Dozer is His responsibility. He established His commands for our well-being. He can have all the commands in place, however, unless we employ them, we can't tap into their life-preserving, joy-giving, freeing power. " … in keeping them (His commands) there is great reward." (Ps. 19:11)

The Command Illuminator, more potent than any Star Wars ray, is available to all God's children. When we seize the constellation of His laws and commands, it floods our path with light, revealing where it is safe to step. Like a laser, the Command *Illuminator* also acts as a Command *Eliminator*, obliterating obstacles.

For example, a few years ago when I put in for a sabbatical leave from my faculty position at the college where I taught, one individual threw huge road blocks in the path of my application. Gigantic boulders, they were, of the Mt. Rainier size. Over a period of several months, at every turn, this person continued to thwart my movement forward. Exasperated and angry, I wrote a scathing email to this woman. Before I hit "send," the Lord breathed a portion of Scripture into my mind. Honestly, at this moment, I do not recall the actual verse, but I do remember the impact of the bidding to pray for her rather than transmit the message. Several weeks later, the Board of Trustees granted me a year off with partial pay. Am I ever glad for the Command Illuminator-Eliminator!

Have you ever dared to run with your eyes closed? It would take complete faith, absolute trust in a smooth, obstacle-free path ahead. When we take hold of the Command Illuminator-Eliminator, we are free to run without stumbling through each day.

Sounds easy enough. And certainly rewarding. But when bad things happen, our basic instinct is to fight or take flight. So, when God exhorts us to thank Him for all things, it goes against our human nature. It conflicts with our desire for control. We want to be in charge of our own Eliminator and zap everything creating havoc. In a sense, this is what we attempt to do by taking revenge, filing lawsuits, yelling, harboring grudges, hating, or similar behaviors. Whether we admit it or not, we all have some behavior we typically resort to when we are wronged. Perhaps it isn't aggressive; maybe it's passive like ignoring someone or killing him with kindness, yet not of the Godly kind.

> "*Change your thoughts and you change your world.*"
> —*Norman Vincent Peale*

In reality, over what situations do we have control? Zero! *Nada!* Zilch! Simply put, the only things we have control over are our thoughts, words, and behaviors in situations and in relationships. Epictetus, a first-century Greek philosopher, wrote in *Epictetus: Discourses and Enchiridion*: " ... some things are in our power, while others are not. In our power are the will, and all voluntary actions; out of our power, the body and its parts, property, parents ... children ... country ... all our fellow beings" (58). In other words, we have control only over our own actions. Nothing else.

Epictetus lived his youth as a slave in Rome. Eventually he was freed and lived a hard life as a cripple. When exiled from Italy, he fled to Greece where he studied and became one of the early century's great thinkers, his life of hardship providing him with great insight. Realizing he could overcome, at least internally, the bad things in life, he stated, "What is it, then, that disturbs and terrifies ... ? What is by nature free cannot be disturbed or restrained by anything but itself; but its own convictions disturb it."[2]

In short, our control lies in our response to what has happened, which in essence, is shaped by the view we have of the situation. When we seize the opportunity to see things from the Lord's perspective and respond as God calls us to do, we extricate ourselves from the control the incident has over us. We may have been a victim of an occurrence, but we can choose to not be spiritually or emotionally victimized.

Perhaps a story of one of my ordeals will help bring this concept into focus. Our home has been robbed numerous times. It's as if neon arrows point out of the sky at our house with the banner, *Come on over. The Stones are giving things away. Help yourself.* I'm ready to post a sign, *You are too late. There's nothing left.*

This last time, (or should I say this most recent time, because how can I be sure it is the *last* time?) I got out of bed, looked out our second story window and watched a white pickup speed out of our driveway, taking $1,400 worth of equipment from our garage. After calling the sheriff, I launched into lament and anger. (Did the thieves steal the lawnmower that wouldn't start? Oh no, they made off with the one that revved right up. How had they known?) God immediately pressed upon me to thank Him for our loss. I gritted my teeth and mouthed the words. Soon, I was praying for the robbers' souls and for anyone who may end up buying the stolen items. It took a little while, but by the end of the day, I was no longer fuming. Praise God, the burglars did not get away with my peace. Thank you, Lord, for illuminating my darkness and eliminating my distress.

Giving thanks is a behavior, which involves choosing to respond or act, even if by only speaking the words. It puts us in control of *ourselves* in the

---

2 *Epictetus: Discourses and Enchiridion* (Based on the Translation of Thomas Wentworth Higginson). (Roslyn, N.Y.: Walter J. Black, Inc., 1944), 52-53.

circumstances as opposed to the circumstances controlling us—and leaves God in control of the situation.

The following episode is similar, yet takes a different twist.

Heather's Story

A woman in her late twenties, Heather, was shopping when she needed to use the furniture store's public restroom. Before washing her hands, she removed her wedding ring and placed it on the counter. Immediately upon pushing through the door to leave, she realized she wasn't wearing the ring and went back in to retrieve it. To her shock and horror, it was gone. Nobody else had gone in or out, and the only other person there was a cleaning lady. Heather asked the woman if she'd seen the ring.

"No, I haven't," the woman replied.

After marching to the manager's office, Heather recounted the experience and asked in so many words, for him to demand the janitor to fork it over. He refused, saying his employee would never steal.

At home, Heather descended into despair. Recently, she had added two bands, each a circlet of small diamonds crowning the top and bottom of the ring. She and her husband had designed it with the plan that when their two young daughters came of age, they would talk with them about the importance of abstinence before marriage—and before God. Since Heather and her husband had refrained from sexual relations before their wedding vows, their desire was to symbolically pass on this legacy by removing the bands and placing the covenant rings onto each of the girl's fingers following a discussion of the value of virtue. The absence of this ring was more than a material loss.

Even in her distress, Heather refrained from cursing the thief. Instead, she followed an urging to "Bless those who persecute you; bless and do not curse." (Rom. 12:14) Although the word persecute didn't quite fit in the literal sense in this instance, the concept was a perfect fit. Heather prayed for whoever took it. She implored the Lord to make His presence known to the woman, so that if this person didn't know God as her personal Savior, as she wore the ring, she would come to Him.

During the next couple of weeks, although she was sorry her ring was gone, Heather had peace; her emotional turmoil had calmed. Even if she never got the ring back, she was able to let it go because of God's grace. Then, she received a call from the store manager. The ring had been mailed to him along with a note saying, "I'm sorry."

Wow! Without the illumination of God's Word—His entreaty for Heather to pray for this woman—and Heather's obedience to do so, I seriously doubt she would ever have retrieved her wedding ring. By obeying, Heather also avoided being snared by a briar of bitterness.

"Blessed are they who keep his statutes and seek him with all their hearts."—Psalm 119:2

Although my husband and I never did retrieve anything pilfered from our property, by grasping the full power of God's commands, Heather and I share a similar outcome—revival of the soul.

Revival of the Soul

Someone asked me what revival of the soul is, what it feels like. Ladies, have you ever experienced that state of euphoria when menstrual cramps cease? I'm not sure this is the best example; but it's the first that came to mind. In essence, revival of the soul is the absence of pain—in the mental, emotional, and spiritual sense—and being elevated into euphoria. Dictionaries define euphoria as a state of well-being. Rapture is also a synonym. Simply put, revival of the soul is when we extricate ourselves from distressing things and move into the presence of God, for there is no other place of absolute well-being.

When I began to anguish over being ripped off again and felt helpless over not being able to do anything about it, (I had gotten a German shepherd, who, by the way, lounged at the side of the driveway, yawning and picking her teeth while watching the robbery go down), I started to plummet into a state of distress. Granted, it was only momentary, since God immediately intercepted my downward spiral by instructing me to thank Him. But even spending a short-lived stretch in emotional gloom is more time in darkness than the Lord wants for us. Just as Peter amazingly walked on water until he got his eyes off Jesus, so I began to sink when I raged at the thieves and our loss of property. Praise the Lord, He didn't let me sink to the depths!

Perhaps a more fitting example of revival of the soul is what being caught up in awesome praise and worship music does for us. Think back to the last time you were lifted right out of your seat and into the presence of God as you and others sang songs of celebration and reverence to our Lord and Savior. Can you recall your state of well-being? At that point, were you mentally planning what you were going to cook for dinner? Or wondering if you forgot to turn off your curling iron? Or worrying about whether or not it would rain before you could mow the lawn? No. Your total focus was on Jesus. Close your eyes and draw close to Him right now. Sing praises to Him. Immerse yourself in His presence. Let Him revive your soul before reading further.

Fix Your Eyes Upon Jesus

When I was a child, every Sunday morning I joined my Grandmother Muckel on the second pew in Bloomington, Nebraska's little white clapboard church. On the front wall to the side of the altar, hung a large picture of Jesus carrying a lamb beside a pasture stream. I loved to imagine I was that lamb in His arms. And I loved to sing about Jesus. Even now I can recall Grandma's soprano voice sliding up and down the scales to reach each note. One particular hymn, "Turn Your Eyes Upon Jesus," encouraged me to focus on Him and the loving look on His face as he carried the lamb. As I did, things around me dimmed, just as the song promised. I couldn't put a name to it then, but now I know those were times of revival of my soul—when I began to trust in Him. This foundation of trust later helped me to thank Him for all things.

Although I have loved Jesus as far back as I can remember, I didn't give my life to Him until I was in my thirties. Actually, I didn't know about the plan of salvation until I became an adult, for the church I attended as a child taught that as long as we were good and tried hard to do things right, we would go to heaven. I marvel at Christ's faithfulness to me over the years and at how He prepared me to come to the truth that His law is perfect. I'm glad my salvation didn't depend upon me being good enough. If that were the case, His law would definitely be flawed because I am imperfect. Hallelujah for the perfect—and only—way to get to heaven: through accepting Jesus, who is perfect, as Savior! That's enough to revive a person's soul right there.

God's law and commands are flawlessly designed to bring about revival, which is vital for our spiritual life and for our growth. David so wonderfully captured the essence and benefits of the Lord's commands in Psalms 19:7-11. I hope this chart helps you get a clear picture of how much He loves you and what blessings He has for you as you embrace His commands.

Life-Giving Results of God's Law:

Law of the LORD is →	perfect & →	revives our souls
Statutes of the LORD are →	trustworthy & →	make us wise
Precepts of the LORD are →	right & →	give joy to our hearts
Commands of the LORD are →	radiant & →	give light to our eyes
Fear of the LORD is →	pure & →	endures forever
Ordinances of the LORD are →	sure, righteous,	
	precious, sweet & →	give warning, great reward

༄

Meditate on Your Favorite Scriptures

As you ponder these truths, please record Bible verses hidden in your heart, verses which have ministered to you, lifted you, rescued you, or breathed spiritual, mental and emotional life back into you. They will continue to revive your spirit.

I. Scripture Address: _____

   Verse:_____

   _____

   _____

   _____

   _____

2. Scripture Address: _____

   Verse:_____

   _____
   _____
   _____
   _____

3. Scripture Address: _____

   Verse:_____

   _____
   _____
   _____
   _____

4. Scripture Address: _____

   Verse:_____

   _____
   _____
   _____
   _____

5. Scripture Address: _____

   Verse:_____

   _____
   _____
   _____
   _____

6. Scripture Address: _____

   Verse:_____

   _____

   _____

   _____

   _____

7. Scripture Address: _____

   Verse:_____

   _____

   _____

   _____

   _____

Record instances when the Command Illuminator-Eliminator worked powerfully in your life, clearing the path for your more trouble-free and safe journey:

☙

Invitation to Personal Prayer

Thank you, Father God, for your life-giving Word. It truly does level
my path.

Memory Verse

"I will walk about in freedom, for I have sought out your precepts."
Psalm 119:45

~5~

The Way to Wisdom

"The statutes of the LORD are trustworthy, making
wise the simple."
Psalm 19:7

Do you believe God? I don't mean do you believe *in* God, for even demons do that and shudder. Rather, do you trust that what He says in His Word is true? Do you believe He gives us commands, i.e. directions, because He wants what is best for us? If you answered yes, then you know in all things God is working for you and for your good because you love Him and are called according to His purpose. (Rom. 8:28)

God sees what will happen when we don't follow his commands. He wants to steer us away from possible harmful consequences. He doesn't want us to get hurt when we veer off the path His commands have cleared for us.

What about when we don't follow God's commands? Does He still work for our good? Can He still bring us into a position of realizing that His commands are trustworthy? Can understanding and wisdom possibly result from our sin?

Have you made a mistake and then found yourself in the midst of chaos or tragedy? When we're in the midst of the storm, whether as a result of our own choices or not, it is difficult to see through the pain and torment and is seemingly impossible to believe at that moment things are working for our good.

Fear of God is the beginning of wisdom. This type of fear is not the kind where we tremble in dread but where we have such a reverence for God that everything around us fades in the light of His glory. Wisdom is looking at things through God's point of view. When we walk in the path of His commands, we begin to see what God sees.

As Claire relates her story as told to me, it is hard to see how God is working for her good. And yet …

Claire's Story

I was dying inside.

My marriage was like living with a roommate. I felt anonymous, neglected. I longed for love and security and companionship and all those things a marriage should have. I tried to talk with my husband about this on numerous occasions. I wrote letters to him. I did everything I could to get him to realize a whole piece of me was missing. I wanted him to realize we couldn't continue our relationship the way it was. The last time I went to him, I was bawling. I got down on my knees; he was in bed. I said, "I hurt so bad inside. I feel so lonely. I can't continue like this. I'm willing to do anything."

He didn't respond.

I told him I was going to have an affair. He asked if I was threatening him. I said, "No. This is what I'm going to do because I'm so empty and lonely. I can't live like this. I'm telling you, if we don't do something, I'm afraid of what's going to happen. I'm begging you to get help."

He laughed.

It would've been better if he'd stabbed me with a knife; it would have hurt less. That was the turning point for me. I did have an affair; what I was doing was wrong. I told my husband. I was dead inside.

Even though he hadn't been before, my husband became abusive—physically, sexually, emotionally. He used my kids as a weapon. The situation escalated and got worse. An avid hunter, he would say things like, "How long do you think I can sit and wait to get you in the crosshairs of my gun? One day … BAM! You'll never know it's coming. I can outwait you. I have more patience."

For four of the last six weeks of being in that house, he held me hostage. We lived in the country, at the end of a long road. I couldn't go anywhere because I had three kids: a disabled son who couldn't walk, a baby, and our oldest child who was five. My husband unplugged the phones and took them with him when he went to work. He fixed the vehicles so I couldn't drive. He threatened me, threatened the kids. He told me he would kill us. I believed him.

He wrote out contracts and made me sign them. Things like, "I will never see my friend, and I will never again speak to the man with whom I had the affair. I am going to quit school and never go back." Then he said, "This is going to hold up in court."

It was terrible. He made me do things—never anything involving our children, thank heavens. But horrible things I'm too ashamed to speak of. He would set up situations and make me respond in a certain way. Then he would point to me and say, "I'm going to take this to court and you'll never get your kids. They'll know you're a freak." I didn't know he was videotaping until after. It was very incriminating, but it didn't show the context. It didn't show what happened before or what happened after, so it actually looked like I was absolutely a raving maniac. That went on for about four weeks. I didn't get to call anybody. I could talk to no one.

People who don't understand this kind of abuse probably wonder why I didn't just leave. What happens to prisoners of war is exactly what happened to me. Looking back on it now, I think, *No way. This could never happen because I'm so strong.* I now realize we're all vulnerable to mind control. I was totally helpless.

To tell you how far gone I was, he would hold a gun to my head and tell me to pull the trigger. I would do it. And then he would laugh and say "Next time I'm going to put bullets in it." But the gun was nothing compared to the strongest weapon ever. He had my children. He was going to hurt my kids. The constant threat, imminent threat ....

Four weeks into this hostage situation, people had been trying to call me, but he wouldn't let them speak to me. Not even my dad. My friend called and said, "You better let me speak to Claire right now or I'm going to call the Sheriff."

He'd say, "She's in the bathroom, or she just went to the store—or whatever." Finally, he let me talk to her. I don't remember much of the phone call; I was in such a daze. Thirty minutes later my friends were in my driveway. My husband freaked out because they said they were either going to take me or call the cops. They took me. He wouldn't let them take the kids. When I got out of there, I had bruises all over my body from his abuse.

He filed for divorce and set out to systematically destroy me. My family, my friends—even though they'd seen the bruises—everybody believed what he told them. My father, my stepmother, my sister, my best friend—all of them turned on me and supported him. My best friend of ten years told me it was because I had had an affair and she needed to find a way to be righteous before God. The only way she could do that was to punish me for my sins. My dad didn't join them but didn't do anything to stand up for me.

I knew the moment I went into court I was going to lose my kids. The Family Court guy, a respected member of my husband's church, implied that because I'd had an affair I didn't deserve to be a mother or have my children. Family Court had requested an MMPI—a psychological inventory—so we both had one. When I was administered the test, the secretary handed it to me. I never saw that psychologist before, during, or after. It came back that I was loony-toons and my husband was sane.

> *"Blessed is the man who always fears the* LORD, *but he who hardens his heart falls into trouble."*—*Proverbs 28:14*

Seven years later when I petitioned to get my oldest daughter out of her father's house, my appointed Attorney General for the State of Colorado said, "You have to get another MMPI because this one looks terrible."

"No way. I'm not doing another one of those because I used to think I was pretty sane until that came back saying I was nuts," I told him.

The Attorney said, "This was administered by Dr. So & So—a psychologist known to say anything to whoever pays him."

I agreed to take another MMPI with a different psychologist. I was extremely apprehensive, scared spitless because here I was trying to get my daughter out of her father's house and I'm going to be nuts and Emily's going to be sent to live with the Addams family somewhere.

When I met with the new psychologist, he asked why I was taking it again. I said, "I don't want to speak to you about that. I don't want to tell you anything that will give you any preconceived ideas. I want to take this for what it's worth, with no conversation about history." I took it and met with him for a follow-up. It turned out not only am I not crazy, I am very much not crazy. This psychologist was astonished at what had initially taken place. In the end, the first psychologist's report is what had made me lose the kids. When the second psychologist submitted his report, he was blatant in letting it be known that under no circumstances should an MMPI be administered without first meeting with the client.

What happened to me in that house subsequently happened to my kids. Emily got out when she was thirteen. I live with that. The kids used to call me, having sneaked the phone into the bathroom. "Mommy, you have to help us. Mommy, get us out of here. Mommy, help," they would plead. I was sitting in a house twenty miles away unable to move while my kids begged me to help them, and I couldn't. He used the one thing that had the most power to control me—my kids. Even though I talk about this in the past, it's every bit as fresh now as it was then.

Murder would have been more humane than having my children torn from me. They are part of me. The day my friends freed me from my hostage situation, I was in no shape to fight for them. I had no power. Death would have been better than what I went through. If my ex-husband had honestly felt they were better off with him … if he really loved them … but he didn't. He used them as a weapon to destroy me. Two years after losing my kids, I prayed to God for strength to kill myself. I remember sitting in the bathtub with a gun to my head and a blanket over me to contain the mess.

I wanted my son and daughters back but knew I would never get them. Today, I admit my reasons were partly selfish—to prove I am a good person and mom. I wasn't looking at it from God's view. I honestly thank God now that my children went to live with my ex-husband. I believe that if I'd gotten custody, he would have killed us all.

Here it is umpteen years later, and he is still threatening me. Just two weeks ago he said, "It may not be today, tomorrow, or a year from now, but some day you'll walk outside and see a red dot right here." He pointed to his forehead between his eyes and went, "BAM!"

Some day I will know why I have endured all of this. I have no doubt I'll be able to say, "It is for this moment I have experienced these horrific things."

❦

Toward the end of my interview with Claire, her daughter, Emily, in her early twenties, joined us. I asked Emily if she is bitter or angry about what she has gone through.

She answered, "No. I used to live inside myself. Several times I thought about ending my life. Then I found two people who believed my story. I learned to speak out. It took courage to meet with social workers and attorneys, and go through the court system. I wouldn't be who I am now if I hadn't gone through all that I have. I like who I am today."

Claire and Emily have a wonderful, loving relationship. They are indeed best friends.

If wisdom is seeing things through God's perspective, I can't help but wonder what is in God's lens with regards to Claire living day-to-day with her ex-husband's death threats. As I allow myself to speculate, I am immediately reminded of my limited human scope. For I am thinking in terms of snapshots of time. There is the future and eternity to consider.

Claire went on to complete a Bachelor's Degree and earned her Master's in Social Work. This remarkable woman will indeed be able to minister to individuals in need.

Why have I included this story that, at this point, doesn't have a happily-ever-after ending? It is to encourage anyone in the midst of an ordeal that seems hopeless, with no guarantee of victory—at least in a worldly sense. Hope lies in looking beyond present suffering and searching for gains in the process. What has Claire gained? A promise that all will end well? No. Not externally, anyway. Claire's gains are internal. Imagine what courage it takes for her to face each day. Yet in a God-given courage, that no one can steal from her, she puts her hope. It is solid, eternal.

Claire refuses to live in fear of her ex-husband's threats. She embraces Jesus as her Savior, and I believe He will use Claire as a model for other women to push through fear to trust Him.

The way to wisdom for Claire has, indeed, proved to be paved by fear (awesome reverence) of God while steering clear of fear of man.

Grace in the Midst of Sin

Let's face it—we've all disobeyed God's commands at one time or another. Maybe your disobedience wasn't adultery. As you think back, which of God's commands have you broken? Were you the object of gossip and retaliated? Have you ever been jealous of others whose spouses shower them with flowers on special occasions while you receive nary an acknowledgement of Valentine's Day or your birthday? Have you lied to avoid creating hard feelings? Is temptation to coveting neighbor's property something you give in to? We know Satan is more often than not the instigator of these promptings to violate scriptural principles.

In the Grip of Grace, Max Lucado states, "When under attack, our tendency is to question the validity of God's commands." (146) So, it isn't just against Satan that we wrestle. Our carnal desires crop up when we want what we want when we want it. Even in the midst of our prayers, we often believe we know what is best, and disregard God's sovereignty. When His designs for us interfere with our plans and desires, we doubt God has only good in store for us.

Do you suppose when God told Eve not to eat from the tree of knowledge of good and evil that she thought, *Hmm. He just doesn't want me to have any of the good stuff*? Or, after the serpent got through with her, *God doesn't want us to be wise*.? Or perhaps she didn't want to believe God's warning was for her own protection.

How about Lot's wife? When the angels ushered her, along with her family, out of town and warned her not to look back because the Lord was going to destroy Sodom and Gomorrah, what might she have been thinking? *Oh, come on. Like that's really going to happen.* Did she turn to see if God really meant what He said? Maybe she was simply curious. The point is, she disobeyed God's command and paid for it with her life. If only she had believed the command was for her own protection! (Gen. 19)

Everyone, at one time or another, comes to the juncture where (s)he veers off the path of God's commands. Sometimes we arrive at a destination of few consequences. Other times, we find ourselves in the thickest of dark clouds. Can you imagine how God's heart aches at what Claire has endured and continues to endure at the hands of her ex-husband? Thank heavens our Lord loves us—His children—so much that He keeps no record of wrongs. (1 Cor. 13:5) This includes even Claire's ex-husband if indeed he has given, or will give, his life to Christ.

Although the Lord's grace and mercy pick us up, dust us off, and set us back on Wisdom Way, how much easier it would be for us to never leave the path of His commands in the first place.

King David's Choice and Consequences
Like Claire but for a different reason, King David committed adultery....

One evening in a stroll around the roof of his palace, David spots a stunning woman bathing in a pool below. David already has several wives, but he sends for this beautiful woman. Bathsheba is brought to him and he sleeps with her even though she is married to Uriah, one of his soldiers who is away at war.

So when Bathsheba sends word that she is pregnant, they both know the baby is David's. David orders Uriah home from the battlefield so Uriah will be thought to be the father of this child. Uriah returns to Jerusalem but rather than going home to Bathsheba, sleeps at the palace entrance. Why? Because he is concerned that his comrades in arms are sleeping in tents in an open field, and he can't justify his own comfort and pleasure. What a man of honor! The next night David gets Uriah drunk so he will go home and sleep with Bathsheba. Again, Uriah does not go home. By now, David is sweating arrows because he knows he and Bathsheba can be put to death because of the law against adultery. So what does he do? He orders Uriah to the battlefront where he knows the enemy is strongest. Uriah is killed, and David is off the hook. Or is he?

Nope. Even though God sends Nathan, one of David's prophets, to tell him the Lord has taken away his sin and that he isn't going to die, David suffers the consequences of his actions. David loses his and Bathsheba's son to death and his wives end up sleeping with his best friend.

All along David knew God's commands were trustworthy. David's Psalms are filled with this knowledge and acclamation. He knew Old Testament laws were designed to direct people to get right with God. Directly after the death of his infant son, David yielded to God's statutes, entering once again into a sanctuary of trust and righteousness. David knew God would use His precepts to make him wise, putting it in these words: "Surely you desire truth in the inner parts; you teach me wisdom in the inmost place." (Ps. 51:6) Truly God's commands are the way to wisdom!

Although we cannot work for mercy and forgiveness because Jesus is our covering for sin, God's commands are not only about us getting right with Him but about getting right with ourselves as well. Do you recall how miserable you felt in your spirit at each sin you have committed? One way of getting right with ourselves is not to thank God for the sin we have just perpetrated but to thank Him for the consequence of it. For it is in the consequences that we are reminded that if we hadn't gotten off the path in the first place we wouldn't be in this place of pain or suffering.

The Gate to Wisdom Way

Have you strayed off the path of God's commands? Do you need a clearly cut road back onto Wisdom Way? Ephesians 5:20 is a gate. Thank God for the consequences of your sin. Remember, you don't have to *be* thankful for the cost of your wrongdoing. For just as King David gained wisdom and Claire received courage and the insight that she and her children were still alive as a result of her not getting custody of them, you also will reap a harvest of God's perspective—and peace.

As you trust in the Lord and don't try to understand things from your point of view, He will make your paths straight. (Prov. 3:5) Part of this path straightening comes via the wisdom we gain by seeing things from God's perspective. King Solomon captured the sum total of staying on the path of God's commands ... or not ... when he wrote "Understanding is a fountain of life to those who have it, but folly brings punishment to fools." (Prov. 16:22)

Just before Paul spoke of knowing the secret of contentment, he wrote about prayer and thanksgiving. Surely this is how he arrived at this understanding: "... I have learned to be content whatever the circumstances ... I have learned the secret of being content in any and every situation ... I can do everything through him who gives me strength." (Phil. 4:11-13) While union with Christ is the key to contentment, giving thanks to God for all things was Paul's secret of "being" in that place of perfect union, of "being" content. I wonder if he learned this lesson upon being blinded on the road to Damascus when Jesus appeared and asked Paul why he was persecuting Him. (Paul was responsible for the murder of many Christians.) Is it possible Paul realized that this sudden sightlessness was a consequence of his previous blind eye to Christ's message? Could it be, from the very beginning of his conversion that during his three days' loss of sight, Paul thanked God for it? If so, he would have come to understanding one of the most powerful principles of restoration.

> *"A successful person is one who can lay a firm foundation with the bricks that others throw at him or her."*—David Brinkley

Although we can't be certain that Paul thanked the Lord for his blindness, we do know Paul aspired to know Christ and His redeeming power. God provided Paul with ample opportunity to "get there." Through adversity. Time after time, Paul was thrown into prison. Instead of getting caught up in his circumstances—rats, dark dungeons with wrist-and-ankle-biting chains, and starvation—rather than concentrating on his pain, he focused on his Lord and Savior. Additionally, Paul prayed for his jailers. God opened a door of opportunity for Paul ... a door which Paul walked through with a heart of praise and thanksgiving. As a result of taking this path, Paul opened doors for his guards as well, who in turn were set free into the knowledge of the saving grace of Jesus Christ.

We, too, can not only endure but become victors in whatever our circumstances through Christ who gives us strength and wisdom. In fact, He tells us that we can be *more* than conquerors through Him because He loves us! (Rom. 8:37)

Truly, the statutes of the Lord are trustworthy and do make us wise.

 ## Invitation to Personal Reflection

Reflect on times you veered off the path of God's commands.

Like Eve, was one of these a time when you believed there really wasn't any harm in partaking of something that looked good? What was this forbidden fruit?

What consequences did you suffer?

Like Lot's wife, was there an occasion when you didn't believe God's warning was for your own protection?

What was the outcome of your decision to ignore the Lord's counsel?

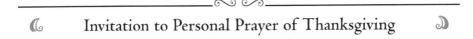

Invitation to Personal Prayer of Thanksgiving

Lord, I thank you for each of these consequences. (Name them one by one.) I am trusting that by thanking you for all that I have endured, you will help me see things from your perspective. By seeing things as you do, I will be better able to keep my feet firmly planted on the path of your commands. Thank you for loving me so much and wanting only good for me. Amen.

Memory Verse

"Teach me knowledge and good judgment, for I believe in your commands."
Psalm 119:66

6

The Joy of the Lord Is Our Strength

"The precepts of the LORD are right, giving joy
to the heart."
Psalm 19:8

Nebuchadnezzar broke down Jerusalem's wall and burned its gates. Inside the city, houses lay in ruin. The Jewish remnant which survived exile and now returned to Jerusalem was in great trouble, for the lack of a city wall left the Israelites defenseless against their enemies. Nehemiah set about rebuilding the wall and gates amidst great opposition. In spite of attacks day and night, with the help of God, he and his countrymen completed the daunting task in fifty-two days!

When the Israelites at last settled into their homes, they assembled at the Water Gate to hear a reading from the Book of the Law of God. People wept at the words, recognizing the significance of their sins. For too long they had disobeyed the commands, decrees, and laws God had given Moses. As such, they had suffered much. At this weeping, Nehemiah stepped forth and said, "Go and enjoy choice food and sweet drinks, and send some to those who have nothing prepared. This day is sacred to our LORD. Do not grieve, for the joy of the LORD is your strength." (Neh. 8:10)

Nehemiah's message declared that the Israelites' tears signified the end of a period of disobedience—that because of their repentance, they were now restored unto the Law. And within the Law they would know the joy of the Lord, which would be their strength.

King David recognized that God had designed His Law for just this purpose—to bring people out of grief into joy through His life-giving statutes, i.e. His decrees, His commands. David reveled in this promise and hope, as evidenced in his proclamation, "Your statutes are my heritage forever; they are the joy of my heart." (Ps. 119:111) What an inheritance!

I wonder if most Christians realize the enormity of this legacy. When I gave my life to Christ, I savored my salvation. The promise of eternal life wrapped me in a blanket of comfort and security. But I had no awareness of the additional treasure that was now mine—God's statutes. I was ignorant of the fact that His commands were there to protect and guide me.

It was in the final semester of my Master's Degree in Counseling that I accepted Jesus as my Savior. My secular training had prepared me to have unconditional positive regard for clients, and through this channel I would guide people toward emotional health and happiness. I recall a professor making it clear that I was not to judge or impose my values upon clients. I asked him, "But what if they are living immorally?"

"That is not for you to decide," he replied. "It is up to you to validate their feelings and support that which makes them happy."

Yikes! I realized even in my counseling infancy that there is no way to "live wrong" and "feel right." Eventually a person's conscience, via the Holy Spirit, will convict him or her of treading down an unsafe path. Initially, rationalization and justification keep us from admitting wrongdoing, but sooner or later we come face to face with our choices. And when they stare back at us, we can no longer hide from the consequences. Without rules to live by, we have no North star by which to navigate through calm or troubled waters.

Your statutes are my delight; they are my counselors. (Ps. 119:24)

A short while after I became a Counselor, I realized God's purpose for leading me into this profession. As wounded individuals come, I listen, provide a safe place for them to express emotions, help them identify healthy behaviors, and teach that they cannot change the past but can change their response to it. I help them let go of bitterness, anger, and other harmful mental states, offer Scriptures as comfort and guidance—and pray. The rest is up to God.

How do God's statutes, or commands, act as a counselor? Hebrews 4:12 tells us "For the word of God is living and active. Sharper than any double-edged sword, it penetrates even to dividing soul and spirit, joints and marrow; it judges the thoughts and attitudes of the heart."

In counseling, it is vital to unearth clients' true feelings, thoughts, and motives. Yet, I am not always able to accomplish this for several reasons. Perhaps the client hasn't come to fully trust me. Maybe (s)he isn't in touch with these things. It might be because the client doesn't want to be accountable, or doesn't want to change. Whatever the reason, I can do only so much. On the contrary, God's Word is alive and powerful. With it He convicts us of our wrongdoing, bad attitude, tight grip on bitterness, anger, anxieties, etc. Our Lord is the Divine Physician. He uses His Word to cut away that which keeps us from running with a free heart.

"If anger consumes you and you can't extricate yourself from its clutches—even though you have tried such strategies as counseling and asking God for deliverance—and you still have no reprieve, then thank God for the situation which ignited your wrath. It's like lining up fury in the crosshairs of your spiritual weapon of giving thanks and pulling the trigger."—MaryEllen

Have you ever wondered how and why Paul was able to be such a joyful prison camper? Chained in dark, dank dungeons, starved, verbally and physically assaulted, and shipwrecked, still, he maintained joy. How "in the world" was he able to do this?

Paul wrote: "Be joyful always, pray continually; give thanks in all circumstances, for this is God's will for you in Christ Jesus." (I Thess. 5:16)

Having Joy vs. Being Joyful

Having joy comes with having Jesus in our lives. Years ago, even though married with two pre-school children, I can honestly say I didn't have joy. It's hard to explain because I was happy, enjoyed my family, and yet lacked something in my soul and spirit. It wasn't until I asked Jesus to come into my life that I experienced real joy, although at the time I didn't identify it as such. My five-year-old niece, however, called it exactly that when—after hearing me present the plan of salvation, without mentioning the word joy—she accepted Christ. "Oh, Aunt Mary," she exclaimed, "I have joy in my heart!"

This is the strength of which Nehemiah spoke.

Can we have joy even in the midst of tragedy? Absolutely, because Jesus never leaves us nor forsakes us; therefore His joy remains in us. Is it human nature to *be* joyful in the eye of a storm? Certainly not for most of us. So what was Paul's secret of being joyful? A joyful state of mind is like a seed we must cultivate. This requires planting, watering, weeding, and harvesting. I believe Paul recognized contentment as the seed which will sprout into joy. In Chapter 4 of Philippians, he offers insight into how we can reap a harvest of contentment. Each step Paul presents is ripe with wise counsel.

Steps to Contentment

1. Rejoice
2. Let your gentleness be evident to all
3. Do not be anxious about anything
4. Prayerfully petition God with thanksgiving
5. Think about whatever is:
   - True
   - Noble
   - Right
   - Pure
   - Lovely
   - Admirable
   - Excellent
   - Praiseworthy
6. Put into practice these things

Paul was way ahead of his time. Today, these concepts are a vital element of the secular world's Positive Psychology—focusing on what is going well in our lives. As a Christian Counselor, I see tremendous wisdom in the guidance Paul provides for our emotional, mental, and spiritual well-being. Please join me in applying these steps.

The Christian Version of Positive Psychology

Step 1: Rejoice in the Lord always.

Close your eyes, if you would, and rejoice in the Lord in your own way, whether it be through song, lifting your hands, kneeling, shouting, crying, or whatever. Revel in the presence of the Lord before moving on to the next step.

Step 2: Let your gentleness be evident to all.

Is your gentleness visible? Imagine a time when you were most gentle. Relax and recall this state of being. Recapture what your body language demonstrated. Calm your thoughts. Taking every thought captive to Christ helps. How do you do this? By turning your thoughts toward Jesus and our Heavenly Father's world of wonders. Dwell in His presence. In His love. Let this transport you to a gentle place.

Step 3: Do not be anxious about anything.

This certainly is easier said than done.

I'm reminded of the story of a woman who kept thinking of pink elephants. When told to get the pink elephants out of her mind, it only reinforced the image. She tried not to think pink. Pink ballooned in her thoughts. She tried not to think elephants, yet the beasts multiplied as mental fixtures filling head space.

The harder you try not to be anxious, the more entrenched anxieties become.

If you could put a face and shape to the anxiety that attaches to you in times of stress or worry, what would it look like? How big is it? It is easier to deal with the tangible rather than the abstract. So, go ahead, visualize anxiety if you can. Now that you have a clear picture, you are in a position to take hold of it. Imagine kicking anxiety to the curb. Or better yet, place it in Jesus' lap. Leave it with Him.

> *"Fretting springs from a determination to get our own way."*—*Oswald Chambers*

Step 4: Present your requests to God with thanksgiving.

This involves changing the way we perceive what we ask the Lord for. What request have you made recently? Perhaps your washing machine is on the fritz. A common petition would be, "God, please send someone to repair my machine." Or "Lord, please help me find a washer on sale."

Paul encourages us to ask with thanksgiving. It looks something like this, "Lord, thank you that I am in a position to turn to you for help. Thank you for telling me I can ask for anything. Right now my dirty clothes are piling up. So, please help me with my washing machine predicament, and thanks ahead of time for helping me take care of it."

Step 5: Think about whatever is true, noble, right, pure, lovely, admirable, excellent, and praiseworthy.

I have created my *Whatsoever* list (per the *King James Bible*) and keep it handy to counteract anxiety, pain, and other not-so-welcome intruders. If you wait to throw your list together in a time of need, you'll likely become anxious about generating one. Either that or your mind will hop onto rabbit tracks, flitting here and there, thus defeating the whole purpose of this exercise.

A key to not be anxious about anything is to redirect your thoughts away from what makes you anxious and to replace those thoughts with something positive. In the case of the woman's stampeding pink elephants, when she substituted yellow and brown-spotted giraffes, she was able to eradicate the elephant herd. Perhaps a gaggle of giraffes may not be any better than a bunch of elephants, but the principle of substitution is sound.

For example, on a warm summer evening, my husband and I were enjoying a relaxing stroll in the park when we came upon a disgusting scene. I immediately averted my eyes but the image had already impressed itself in my mind. As I am a visual learner, pictures take root in my brain. As we continued our walk, the incident ran in my head like a looping video. No matter how I tried to suppress it or shake it off, it played again and again. Then I remembered the principle of substitution and a scene from my *Whatsoever* list—a sunset bursting on the horizon in a cascade of brilliant shades of nectarine and cherry. I dwelled on the rich hues of this amazing sight God created for our pleasure, and in this case, for my deliverance. To this day, Satan will sneak in and attempt to evoke that disgusting park episode into my thoughts. Without hesitation, I switch on the sunset, and am tucked under the protection of God's wings.

One way to take every thought captive to Christ is to think about things that are lovely, pure, etc. A *Whatsoever* list is a great way to exterminate worries crawling around inside your head.

Following is an example of a few of the things on my list. When I dwell on a mental image instead of niggling thoughts, my heart and mind are calmed. I encourage you fill in the empty lines with items that come to your mind.

Whatsoever List—One Way to Take Every Thought Captive to Christ

Whatsoever things are:

- **True:**
  - *Jesus loves me!*—I picture myself walking with Him in a flower garden in the early morning's dew. I drink in the peace of His presence. The song, "In the Garden" plays in my thoughts and I am actually there with Him in spirit.
  - *God promises a bright future.* (Jer. 29:11)—The thought and truth of this lifts me out of my present circumstance.

  What truths speak to you?

  _____

  _____

- **Noble:**
  - *Towering fir branches reaching to the sky.*—I envision them praising the Creator. I sense the grandeur, the beauty of creation.
  - *My grandchild telling the truth about breaking something.*—A smile crosses my face at the knowledge that Godly training has taken root.

  What do you imagine as noble?

  _____

  _____

- **Right:**
  - ○ *Americans' responses to hurricane and flood victims, at home and worldwide.*—This Scripture comes to mind: "For I was hungry and you gave me something to eat, I was thirsty and you gave me something to drink, I was a stranger and you invited me in, I needed clothes and you clothed me, I was sick and you looked after me, I was in prison and you came to visit me. ... whatever you did for the least of these brothers of mine, you did for me." (Matt. 25:35-36, 40) What a privilege to do for Jesus!
  - ○ *My marriage of forty years.*—I dial up memories of good times, funny instances. I laugh aloud at the image of my husband shocking me with a broad and grotesque smile of false-Billy-Bob-teeth. His sense of humor and playfulness has kept our marriage on the right track.

What is right in your life?

_____

_____

- **Pure:**
  - ○ *Baby's angel hair.*—With my eyes closed, even now I can feel the softness of the air-light, fuzzy wisps of my grandbabies' hair against my lips. *That was then ... now their teenage hair is gelled and sprayed and stiff.* I chuckle, shake off this thought, and return to their purity at birth.
  - ○ *Mountain streams at the source of melting.*—I can hear the babbling, feel the cool mist, see clear water tumbling over sun-glistened rocks.

What do you identify as pure?

_____

_____

- **Lovely:**
  - ○ *The moon at night shining off a meandering river.*—I see the stark contrast of shimmering light against velvet black and hear the soothing music of running water.
  - ○ *Autumn leaves in an explosion of reds, yellows, and brown.*—I fill my lungs with air and can fairly smell the crisp Fall day. Brilliant colors of bronze, amber, and crimson dance in a breeze that lifts my spirit heavenward.

What that is lovely comes to your mind?

_____

_____

- **Admirable:**
  - ○ *Hummingbirds in stationary flight.*—Such tiny bodies hovering in mid-air; I marvel at their ability to maintain position. Their dive-bombing antics at one another at the feeder make me laugh.
  - ○ *Sarah, my German shepherd's faithfulness.*—She nuzzles my hand for attention. I relish her companionship.

What do you admire?

_____

_____

- **Excellent:**
  - ○ *The intricate weave of a spider's web between flowers, reflecting the sparkle of early-morning mist.*—How delicate are these doilies gracing the furniture of my garden. I am bathed in warm memories of my Grandmother Muckel's crocheted doilies spread over each arm and headrest of every sofa and easy chair throughout her home. Her tattered Bibles lay ready for her reach beside her reading places. From spider webs to Grandmother's love for Jesus and her faithful prayers for my salvation … Mmm … I bask in this Sonshine ….
  - ○ *The awe—and ahhh—of a sunrise.*—Tangerine, peach, and magenta hues flood my mind. The dawn of a new day envelopes me in its soothing embrace.

What do you regard as excellent?

_____

_____

- **Praiseworthy:**
  - ○ *The rush and power of waterfalls proclaiming God's mighty works.*—I had the privilege of visiting Yellowstone National Park and sitting on the landing over one of its waterfalls. The force of the raging river reinforced

our Lord's awesome power. I close my eyes and am there in memory. I am safe and secure in the arms of Christ.

○ *Knowing the sun will come up tomorrow, even if behind the clouds.*—I recall airplane trips above the clouds. The expansive, crystal-clear blue on cotton-ball carpeting lifts me above the storm.

What do you find praiseworthy?

_____

_____

Now that you have your *Whatsoever* list, as Paul instructs us to think on these things, close your eyes and take a few minutes to dwell on the images. Experience the serenity, warmth, and sense of well-being they evoke. In essence, you are taking your thoughts captive to Christ and revering God's creation.

∽

Welcome back from this exercise.

Now that we have our *Whatsoever* list, we are primed for whatever circumstance comes our way and we're ready to:

Step 6: Put all of this into practice

For instance, it's 2 a.m. I can't sleep. A demanding day lies ahead. Rest is imperative. The harder I try to slip into slumber, the more open-eyed I am. Philippians 4 pops into my wide-awake mind....

... Thus, bringing it all together ... step by step:

Step 1: I begin by rejoicing, singing songs of praise—telling Jesus how much I love Him, praising Him for my salvation, His love for me. I realize I've been thrashing about, so I heed the call to gentleness.

Step 2: I fix my thoughts upon God's presence. I imagine the fragrance of His closeness. Soon, I am calmed in body, yet my mind still races with the worries of tomorrow and how badly I need rest.

Step 3: I know I am not to be anxious about anything. I will replace my anxieties with things from my *Whatsoever* list. First, however, I petition God, with thanksgiving, because previous experience has taught me I may not be awake to thank Him before I get through everything on my list. So, I go on to the next step ...

Step 4: "Dear Lord, I want to get to sleep. Thank you that I haven't been able to, for it has caused me to turn to you. Thank you for that. Thank you that you provide the gift of rest. Please bless me with it now."

Step 5. Here I am carried into slumber. I'm not obsessed with proceeding in the order Paul sets out in his verse, so I don't begin with true, noble, or right. I skip to "Pure," close my eyes and concentrate on my first granddaughter as I held her in my arms. Only a few months old, she looked me in the eyes, held my gaze, and gave the most loving smile I've ever received. I am warmed to my core. When I am ready, I move on to "Lovely" and examine delicately woven webs connected between parallel power lines above the road I drive to work. Morning moisture and sun combine to cast diamonds in their lacy nets. The backdrop of the Excellent sunrise in its apricot and fuchsia sky is like a balm unto my soul. I drift away ....

෨෧

Outer Stress, Inner Joy

Fixing my thoughts on and giving thanks for sunrises, flowers, mountain peaks, and such, helps me move into inner peace in Christ and into a field pregnant with joy. For once I am there, it is only a small step to give God thanks for *everything*. As a friend once told me, "Mary, if you get the little things right, the rest will come easier." When God gives commands such as Philippians 4:6-9, to ponder the Noble, Right, Pure, Lovely, Admirable, Excellent and Praiseworthy, and when we follow them, it is easy to see His statutes are delightful and wonderful counsel. Truly, the precepts of the Lord are

"Cana of Galilee ... Ah, that sweet miracle! It was not men's grief, but their joy Christ visited. He worked his first miracle to help men's gladness."—*Fyodor Dostoevsky*

59

right and give joy to our hearts! I am thankful Paul shared the secret of being content in any circumstance.

Just as Paul did, so did David encounter many troubles. And just as Paul never lost his joy, neither did David, as he testified in Psalm 31:7. "I am overcome with joy because of your unfailing love, for you have seen my troubles, and you care about the anguish of my soul." (*New Living Translation*) In fact, David ratchets it up a notch in Psalm 112:7, writing that when a man delights in the Lord's commands, he will not fear bad news. Now that's faith and trust, as opposed to the peace-stealing stool of dread where many of us perch.

God's Promise
"When you obey me, you remain in my love, just as I obey my Father and remain in his love. I have told you this so that you will be filled with my joy. Yes, your joy will overflow!"—John 15:9-11 (*New Living Translation*)

If you cannot identify with this joy, perhaps you haven't completely surrendered to Christ, or something may be blocking the joy of the Lord in your life.

༁

Invitation to Personal Reflection

Reflect on and record when you first recall having joy in your soul and spirit.

_____
_____
_____
_____
_____

How has this joy carried you through tough times? Write out this testimony, not only for your own benefit, but so you can share your testimony as encouragement for those in similar circumstances.

_____
_____
_____
_____
_____
_____
_____
_____
_____

ᥫᨒ

_____ ᥫᨒ _____

《   Invitation to Personal Application   》
_____

The Bible is God's love letter to us. When we personalize His message, we rise to heights beyond measure. Write in your name and situation below.

"Dear _____ , do not be anxious about

_____ .

Instead, thank Me for it. I will give you peace beyond your limited understanding. My peace will guard your heart and your mind in Jesus." –The Lord your God, Who wants to bless and strengthen you.

_____ ᥫᨒ _____

《   Invitation to Personal Prayer   》
_____

Lord Jesus, search my heart and my life. Shine your light on anything
which prohibits me from being filled with your joy. If I have given
Satan a foothold, please reveal that to me. I ask forgiveness for
this and ask for your cleansing blood to restore me unto you.
I surrender my body, soul, and spirit to you. Thank you for
your overflowing joy. Amen.

            Memory Verse

The more you repeat the following memory verse, the more you will embrace the truth of it, and the more empowered you will be to face whatever lies in your path. For as Jesus promised in John chapter 8, verses 31 and 32, "... If you hold to my teaching, you are really my disciples. Then you will know the truth, and the truth will set you free."

"As pressure and stress bear down on me, I find joy in your commands."
Psalm 119:143 (*New Living Translation*)

~7~

Light Pierces Our Darkness

" … The commands of the LORD are radiant, giving
light to the eyes."
Psalm 19:8

"… we also rejoice in our sufferings, because we know that
suffering produces perseverance; perseverance character;
and character, hope. And hope does not disappoint us, because God has poured out his love into our hearts by the
Holy Spirit, whom he has given us."
Romans 5:3-5

Darkness Accentuates Light

Have you ever noticed The Great Masters utilize dark colors to enhance light? Without the blues and blacks, few of 17th-century Dutch artist Rembrandt's masterpieces would have context or form. In his 1644 work of art, "The Woman taken in Adultery," the majority of the canvas is dark. Our eyes are drawn to the figures—the adulteress, her accusers, and Jesus—oil-brushed in light at the bottom center of the painting. It is as if the woman has been lifted from darkness and into Christ's presence. Rembrandt truly captures the power and symbolism of light.

Similarly, God uses the dark times in our lives to show us the bigger picture, to draw us out of the shadows and give shape to who we are and what we are capable of becoming. In light of the redemption the adulteress gained before Christ, I wonder if this woman of the Bible ever gave thanks that her sin was exposed.

Much is written about darkness and light in the Scriptures, and often one is not mentioned without the other. Without darkness, light would exist sans context. Likewise, without light, darkness would have no means of measurement. Because the two are polar opposites, we are afforded more clarity as to the purpose of each.

This contrast is best exemplified at the greatest moment of darkness the world has ever known: "At the sixth hour **darkness** (bold mine) came over the whole land until the ninth hour … With a loud cry, Jesus breathed his last. The curtain of the temple was torn in two from top to bottom." (Mark 15:33-38) Christ's selfless love tore the curtain separating the Holy Place from the Most Holy Place so that we may enter God's very presence—for God is Light. His light pierces a hole in the curtain of our dark circumstances. Without the context of darkness, would we be drawn to the shining light of God's love?

What has separated you from experiencing the freeing power of God's presence? Pain from the past? Dreams shattered? Relationships wrecked? Finances crashed? Have you lost physical abilities or been wrongly accused?

When a veil of darkness drops, we have many choices, some of which are to:

- Succumb and allow it to suffocate and blind us
- Rail against it and let it deplete our energy
- Complain, whine, and moan, "Why me?"
- Blame ourselves and anguish over our failings
- Pray for the Lord's help
- Immediately thank Him for the circumstances

While petitioning the Lord for help is essential, thanking Him is actually the shortest route to the other side of the veil. Praise ushers us into the Most Holy Place. It is here we experience our Creator's awesome presence. David discovered this threshold and revealed the keys to crossing it: "Enter his gates with thanksgiving and his courts with praise, give thanks to him and praise his name." (Ps. 100:4)

In 1898, Margaret J. Harris' house burned to the ground. Even though she had no property insurance, she penned the song, "I Will Praise Him." Despite her ambitions and plans lying in ashes at her feet, she declared she would never cease to praise Him. What a victory for her! Even though all her worldly possessions were gone, she refused to let the darkness of the hour keep her from entering the Most Holy Place.

"The greatest part of our happiness or misery depends on our dispositions and not on our circumstances."
—Martha Washington

As I previously mentioned, when the first revelation of Ephesians 5:20 penetrated my Bible-scanning mind, I wanted to put conditions on it, but God pointed out that His Word says *every* thing, not *some* things.

As a Counselor, I consistently hear stories of trouble, tragedy, and terror. None breaks my heart more than a narrative of the abuse of a child.

As Marcy courageously tells her story in the following pages, you will come to see how her personal application of Ephesians 5:20 to thank God for everything brought her to a higher spiritual intimacy with the Lord, and into a place of healing and peace.

Marcy's Story

My dad began grooming me when I was about two. Mental abuse was intermixed in the sexual abuse, as he threw around lies under the guise of a joke, yet real enough that I had begun to believe if I ever talked about his touching me a lot of bad things would happen. He always promised he would never hurt me, and so having never experienced pain from him, I trusted that as long as I didn't tell anyone what he was doing, I would be safe.

By the time I was a first grader, he was fully sexually abusing me almost nightly. It was then that I saw him as a liar. I began to tell people what he was doing to me. I didn't get the help I thought would come. In fact, the abuse grew worse, with more drastic measures to keep me from remembering the abuse, or ever talking about it again.

65

Then, when I reached the age out of his "target zone," he began to physically abuse me, damaging my body for life. His physical abuse was never out of anger, but was pure manipulation backed up with threats. To secure his image and to erase the previous five years of abuse, he increased the manipulation by stopping all forms of contact with me. This threw me into wanting to get his approval. The further he withdrew, the more I vowed to do whatever it took to get "my daddy" to love me again. Because of the emotional stress and anxiety that I would never again have a relationship with him, I mentally repressed the previous abuse. There was no room in my mind for those recollections anymore; my thoughts were consumed with regaining his love.

One day, he began talking to me. Finally, my life was back to "normal."

When I was sixteen, God began stirring painful childhood memories within me. This marked the beginning of healing. I came out of denial and accepted that I was abused by someone I loved.

As I grew older, I assumed I would go through the healing process with my dad, sisters (who were not abused or do not remember being abused), and Mom. We were very close and although I had read that often bringing something like this out in the open might divide families, I believed my family would be different—we loved each other and nothing could separate us.

I approached them with the truth when I was twenty-four. I was wrong. Healing together was not going to happen. Our relationship was on and off as I sought counseling not only for the abuse, but for their rejection of it as well. I believed it was God's desire for me to remain in a relationship with my family, even though Dad continued to deny what he had done to me.

My family remained my focus. I loved them. My mission was to walk through the healing process with them, and then celebrate a new relationship grounded in truth instead of lies.

When I was twenty-nine, I had a dream.

> *I was in a river with my sisters. We were wading and swimming, having a good time. All of a sudden, my abuser yelled for us to hold on to something, anything. A mudslide was coming. We grasped for branches, rocks, whatever we could find.*
>
> *The sky drew dark. The mudslide came.*
>
> *I held on for as long as I could. The mud got too high. I was too tired. So, I let go.*

The mudslide carried me downstream to a pond. When I stood up, I was clean. I looked around. The sun shone through the trees, and the air was light. I was surrounded by beauty. I was amazed and then I remembered my sisters.

I got out of the pond and ran back up the riverbank. My sisters were still in the mudslide holding on. I yelled, "It's OK. You can let go. I am clean. Look at me! There's a pond; it will catch you. Just let go!"

My abuser yelled from the other side of the river, "She is lying. Hold on. You will die if you let go. Hold on. She is lying."

I knew God was trying to tell me something with that dream. However, I didn't get it. My husband and I began our family. We had three kids one right after the other. We moved across country and continued to see my family as we made trips back and forth.

When my youngest turned one, my parents came to visit. Our children were growing close to the age that I was abused. In order to give me peace, my husband and I finished our basement, adding a guest bedroom and bathroom. Now, at night, when most of my abuse occurred, I could sleep, knowing that an entire floor was between my children and my dad. Neither my husband nor I dreamed my father would attempt to harm our kids. Especially since my family now knew his history of abuse.

While my parents were at my house, my husband and I did whatever we could to make them comfortable. I made their favorite dishes. We served them and expressed our love. I wanted my dad to know, above all, that I forgave him and that I wanted him to experience forgiveness and freedom from his sins. I thought if I could just love him enough, he would want to change, and my sisters and Mom would finally believe me. His admitting the truth now appeared to be the only way for the relationships I had with my family to resume as they used to be. So, I tried hard to reach Dad.

The day I loaded my kids in the van to take my parents to the airport is the day I knew, by looking at my daughter, that something wasn't right. She sat with her blanket over her head while I tried to get to the airport as fast as I could. I was dying to ask her, "What's wrong? What happened?"

I dropped my parents off, and hugged Mom for the last time and said, "I love you." I hugged my dad and looked him in the eye. "I'll be praying for you," I said, and meant it.

I learned from my daughter that my dad did abuse my kids during that trip. My husband and I contacted the authorities. After an investigation, my dad was charged with two counts of indecent liberties with our oldest child, although he had done things to my second child as well.

The wait to go to trial was the lowest point in my life. I could not look myself in the mirror. I dreaded seeing my family in court. Everything I had worked for had blown up in my face. My outreached hand of forgiveness was struck down. I felt stupid and angry with myself for having my parents in our home, and for believing my dad would make the right choice—and for thinking I could control it all.

Godly people helped me through these initial feelings. I was filled with overwhelming sorrow for the losses. I couldn't contain it all. So, I envisioned it leaving my head and going upward to God. This time, I was able to process my pain rather than repress it. I felt it rather than denied it.

In anticipation of court, I knew I was in no way ready spiritually, mentally, or physically to face my family, so I prayed God would use the time for me to grow in Him.

I thought a lot about the dream. I came to understand it was in the pond of peace I was supposed to stay. God never wanted me to leave to do battle with my family. It was His job to convince them of the truth, to save and deliver them. Not mine.

I recorded my thoughts and prayers, an addition to my daily study in God's Word. This birthed my passion for writing. It is therapeutic, healing.

I searched God's Word to figure out why I thought it was my job to save my family. Somewhere along the way, I had picked up this notion, claimed it to be Biblical, and used it as my driving force to heal them. Then I read 1 Corinthians 5, which clearly states that we must hand the sexually immoral over to Satan so that person's sinful nature be destroyed and his spirit be saved. It also is specific about not even eating with such a man.

Plainly, my actions had been opposite of God's instruction. By not knowing His Word or by not claiming it to be relevant in my life today, I had put my children in harm's way, hurt my husband and myself, and possibly delayed my dad's salvation. I explored my misguided steps and realized I had thought so little of myself that I was willing to whitewash what my dad had done to me just so I could keep my family together. I was fighting on the riverbank, and God wanted peace for me. I finally understood.

Waiting for trial was the most fruitful period of my life. I came to a point where I felt ready to be a healed helper, coming alongside others with similar hurts. To help them learn from my mistakes and to offer them the hope we all have in Christ. I learned anything we experience on this earth does not have to be in vain when we have Christ. All of our trials and hurts can be used to make us more like Him. Peace is attainable, real, and exactly God's desire for us, regardless of the storm.

I didn't think it would be possible to live without my sisters, Mom, and my dad. But, isn't it just like God to make the time without them my most productive and peaceful? With God, all things are possible.

Eventually, we had our trial. My husband and I sat in a room with my dad, Mom, and three sisters, none of whom we had spoken to for two-and-a-half years. I was nervous to see them because I didn't know what they would do or say to me. Yet, surrounding us with God's love were seventeen people from our family in Christ. When I felt afraid, I would think *Vanessa is praying for me. Rick is praying for me. Susan is praying for me. Larry is praying for me. Ray is praying for me.* And so on … My family in Christ became my focus. I was lifted up. Such a contrast to my dad, Mom, and sisters.

My dad pleaded guilty to avoid a jury trial. My husband stood and gave a heartfelt speech of forgiveness and love but expressed a deep desire that the truth be dealt with and accepted for the sake of my dad's soul and for all of our relationships.

My dad's lawyer filled the room with accusations. My dad had no new twist to his story; he spoke the same lies—that I had been brainwashed by a counselor, and I had concocted evidence of his sexual abuse.

This time, the false allegations no longer tugged me away from truth. I thought about the preposterous suggestion that I was possessed—and wondered what I was going to do with my dad's words this time around. Like an unwanted gift, I mentally gave them back to the giver. I finally had my identity and genealogy in Jesus Christ. I no longer whitewashed my dad's actions in order to be accepted by my birth family. The truth was clear. I am a child of God, and nothing was going to shake that.

After sentencing, my sisters, Mom, and my dad left quickly. During his fifteen months' probation, my dad received counseling three times a week. I pray it helped.

This trial was no different from previous trials in my life. God used it to help me grow in Him, so I can be free to serve Him. It is no longer about me; it is about Him and His people. My personal desire is to encourage others along the road to recovery and healing. I am living testimony of that healing.

After the court case, during one of my quiet times with God, a water lily came to mind. I thought about how God uses sludge and mire to grow something beautiful and treasured. Was I ready to view my muddy past as fertile soil for who I am today?

When I first considered giving God thanks *for everything*, I listed all the things I had indeed given Him thanks for—including my healing, my children and husband, my comforts. But with further probing and direction towards the things that were not comforts, I journaled, "No, Lord! Please don't ask me to thank you for that. I can't do it. I cannot." In tears and with a lump in my throat, I heard a whisper.

Why?

I resisted the thought that God had any part of my hurt and pain. In the process, I changed His character to fit my image—made Him a victim to the evils of this world, as I was—instead of accepting His sovereignty.

Release came with the realization that I don't need to understand His master plan. As I began to thank Him for each experience, I recognized that harms done to me and those I love are opportunities to learn and grow. In thanking God for the good and bad, I acknowledge who He is and who I am.

I am Marcy, daughter of Abraham and child of God.

Ꮼ

" . . . *when I was a child I spoke and thought and reasoned as a child does.* . . .
Now all that I know is hazy and blurred, but then I will see everything clearly,
just as clearly as God sees into my heart right now."
—I Corinthians 13:11-12 (*The Living Bible*)

If ever there is a testimony confirming "The commands of the LORD are radiant and give light to your eyes," it is Marcy's.

God's Messages of Love, Hope, and Promise

Romans 8:28: "And we know that *in all* (italics mine) things God works for the good of those who love him, and who have been called according to his purpose."

Philippians 1:18-19: " ... I will continue to rejoice for I know that through your prayers and the help given by the Spirit of Jesus Christ, what has happened to me will turn out for my deliverance."

Romans 8:37: " ... in all these things (trouble, hardship, persecution, famine, nakedness, danger, or sword), we are *more* (italics mine) than conquerors through him who loved us."

Psalm 119:71: "It was good for me to be afflicted so that I might learn your decrees."

> *"Thanking God for our painful circumstances allows Him into our wounds. It is like flipping on a light switch in a black room. Light obliterates the dark and suddenly we can see."*
> —*MaryEllen*

The Will of God

- **God's Directive Will**

In the Psalms, David frequently expresses his desire to do God's will and petitions the Lord to teach him His will. In Ephesians, Chapter 5, Paul exhorts us to understand what the Lord's will is. After doing so, Paul spells it out for us, lest we remain uncertain as to what that is. He tells us, rather than fill up on wine, to be filled with the Spirit. We are to communicate one with another with songs and to make music in our hearts.

In his letter to Thessalonica, Paul states God's will is that we be sanctified. Later in the same letter, he writes, "... give thanks in all circumstances, for this is God's will for you in Christ Jesus." (1 Thess. 5:18)

These are just a few verses where God's will for us is revealed.

But what about His will for what happens to us? Why does God allow things that bring harm to self or others?

- **God's Permissive Will**

Because He has given us free will, He has chosen not to "control" us. He does not make us do anything. Rather, He permits us to make our own choices. So, even though He would not want harm to befall us, He allows it because men make mistakes or willfully choose evil. But His Permissive Will isn't the end.

Leslie D. Weatherhead (1893-1976), renowned as one of Britain's finest preachers in his day, authored several books. In *The Will of God*, he identifies three additional categories of God's Will: Intentional, Circumstantial, and Ultimate. (13)

- **God's Intentional Will**

Recently I watched a movie wherein a religious family endured trials, many of these at the hands of a spiteful neighbor. Upon each tribulation, the people would utter, "It is the Lord's will"—even when one of their young men was killed by this neighbor's hired hands.

There are those who truly believe because God is omnipotent, everything that happens is "the Lord's will." Yet, nothing in the Bible supports this belief. On the contrary, as we study the Old Testament, from the get-go we find God attempting to head off disasters. For example, God warned Adam not to eat of the tree of the knowledge of good and evil, for if he did he would die. God's Intentional Will was that mankind would live forever on earth, communing in perfect harmony with Him here.

In fact, throughout Scripture, we see that His Intentional Will is to bless us. "'For I know the plans I have for you', declares the LORD, 'plans to prosper you and not to harm you, plans to give you hope and a future. Then you will call upon me and come and pray to me, and I will listen to you. You will seek me and find me when you seek me with all your heart.'" (Jer. 29:11-13)

- **God's Circumstantial Will**

When we are outside of God's Intentional Will as a result of our actions or others', we move into His Circumstantial Will. Weatherhead defines this as "God's plan within certain circumstances."[3]

---

3 Weatherhead, Leslie D., *The Will of God* (Nashville: Abingdon Press, 1972), 28.

In Marcy's case, God used the sins of her father to be re-channeled into a river of life for her, as opposed to the torrent of death Satan intended. Indeed, Marcy has become a wonderful woman of God. Because of her willingness to thank God for the abuse she endured—being careful to acknowledge it was evil, not the Lord God, that forced incest upon her—Marcy has become a public speaker, helping many wounded women come into the healing power of Christ.

As Weatherhead so aptly states: "And if we can only trust where we cannot see, walking in the light we have—which is often very much like hanging on in the dark—if we do faithfully that which we see to be the will of God in the circumstances which evil thrusts upon us, we can rest our minds in the assurance that circumstances which God allows reacted to in faith and trust and courage, can never defeat purposes which God ultimately wills. So doing, we shall wrest from life something big and splendid. We shall find peace in our own hearts. We shall achieve integration in our own minds. We shall be able to serve our fellows with courage and joy. And then one day—for this has been promised us—we shall look up into his face and understand." (46-47)

- **God's Ultimate Will**

Weatherhead defines God's Ultimate Will as "God's final realization of his purposes." (28)

In the case of Adam and Eve, where God's Intentional Will for them to commune with Him in one accord was not realized because they chose to go against His bidding to avoid eating of the tree of good and knowledge, God did not capitulate. Instead, He conceived

"Flowers grow out of dark moments."—Corita Kent

a plan which would inevitably bring mankind back into His Intentional Will. Jesus would be the bridge via which man could enter back into the Most Holy Place. At the moment when Jesus took the sins of the world upon Himself, paying the price of death, the temple curtain tore, allowing us to enter into God's presence without sin.

So, regardless of whatever wrong choices we make, or whatever harm or evils inflicted upon us that cast us from the Lord's Intentional Will into His

Permissive or Circumstantial Will, we can be assured that ultimately God will work for bringing about what is good for us—bringing us out of the dark into the light!

In the presence of His light we commune with Him in perfect harmony. If our minds are controlled by the Spirit, we have life and peace—harmony with our Creator. Thanking God for allowing trials and heartaches is one way of yielding to the Spirit. Ephesians 5:20 calls us to this thanks giving, for He knows what will bring us peace. Perfect peace.

Hallelujah for the Light that pierces our darkness!

࿉

Invitation to Personal Prayer

Lord God, Creator of the heavens and earth, Creator of me,
thank you for your will for my life. Help me to know
your will and live within it. Amen.

Memory Verse

"Be joyful always, pray continually; give thanks in all circumstances, for this is God's
will for you in Christ Jesus."
I Thessalonians 5:16-18

8

Keeping God's Commands in the Face of Fear

"Peace I leave with you; my peace I give you. I do not give to you as the world gives. Do not let your hearts be troubled and do not be afraid."
John 14:27

"Behold, God is my salvation; I will trust, and not be afraid; for the LORD Jehovah is my strength and my song; he also is become my salvation."
Isaiah 12:2 (KJV)

As a Counselor, I frequently encounter troubled individuals filled with fear. Through my years as a therapist, I have come to understand and recognize the faces and roots of fear.

Fear as a Natural Instinct

God has instilled in us a protective device—an instinct to be afraid. Even babies show fear before they learn to be afraid of things that will harm them.

Sudden loud noises, for example, can send infants into shrieks of terror. This God-given natural reaction prepares us to fight or take flight.

Learned Fear

As we grow and experience life, we learn to fear. When I was ten years old, I was fearless in delivering newspapers ... until a German shepherd attacked me. For many years thereafter, I was afraid of strange, large dogs. Now, while cautious around unfamiliar, big canines, I no longer am shackled by this fear, for God has helped me break free from this fright through a re-learning process. Over the past few years, we have owned three German shepherds and delighted in their companionship. On the other hand, I have never been bitten by a snake but I fear them. (But, hey, that's Biblical. It's in Genesis 3:15.)

What are you afraid of? Spiders? Heights? Speaking in front of an audience? Committing to a relationship? Abandonment? Losing your job? Most of these fears come about because of a harmful or negative experience, if not through your own encounters, then by way of witnessing them in others' lives.

Still, learned fear can be both healthy and unhealthy. Let's take fear of heights, for example. If it paralyzes me to the extent I won't cross a bridge, then it is unhealthy because it prohibits me from getting to where I want or need to go. However, let's say fear of heights doesn't stop me from crossing a bridge. So, I walk across one on a sweltering hot July afternoon. At the top of the arch, I stop and look over the side. The shimmering, blue water below beckons, promising a cool refreshing dip. At this point, a fear of heights is healthy as it protects me from casting caution to the wind in favor of a cool dunk. Thus, learned fear can be both friend and foe, producing fruit that either poisons or prospers us.

Fear of the Lord

When I first became a Christian, I heard about "the fear of the Lord." At the time, it evoked dread in me. Now that I understand more fully, it stirs delight. Studying the Bible has helped me gain an awareness of God's might—of how since the beginning of time His power has both saved and destroyed. In the parting of the Red Sea, God saved the fleeing Israelites yet destroyed the pursuing Egyptian army. When He sent waters to cover the earth, God saved a faithful remnant through Noah, while destroying unfaithful mankind. God consumed Sodom and Gomorrah in flames, yet delivered Abraham and Lot into a land of milk and honey.

Surely, Zechariah presented these historical facts as he instructed young King Uzziah in the fear of the Lord. For the most part of King Uzziah's life, he did what was right in the eyes of the Lord. As long as he was faithful to God, he prospered. The Lord honored Uzziah's obedience with blessings and divine help. However, in later years of reign, Uzziah assumed responsibility for his own success. In his pride, Uzziah had lost his fear of the Lord. He forgot or discounted God's power. Uzziah switched from trusting in God to trusting in self. Consequently, leprosy devoured Uzziah. (2 Chron. 26)

Fearing the Lord equips us to stand firm in His commands, for then we understand His mighty power to save—or destroy. Learned fear of the Lord is our lifesaver in deep waters. Let us examine another man who knew the fear of the Lord, yet whose fear led him into subterranean waters.

Jonah

Jonah had an assignment from God to go to Nineveh and warn its wicked residents of the danger of divine judgment. As an Israelite, Jonah relished his favored standing with God. As such, he knew the Lord's capacity for grace, compassion, and love, and realized that if the Ninevites repented, God would forgive and not destroy them. To Jonah, God's mercy on Nineveh would mean an end to Israel's position as favored children.

As a prophet, Jonah should have known better than to run away from God. But he skedaddled to Joppa and hopped a ship to Tarshish in an attempt to escape the Lord. (Did Jonah really believe he could run away from God's presence? But then, ever since Adam and Eve tried to hide from our Creator, man has endeavored to accomplish this futile feat.)

Once on the ship and out to sea, Jonah must have thought he had it made because he descended into the bowels of the vessel for a snooze in the midst of a mighty storm. As the tempest pitched the craft about, the ship threatened to break apart. To lighten the load, the crew threw cargo overboard. They prayed to their gods but found no reprieve. At last, the captain sought out Jonah and drew him into casting lots to discover who had caused this calamity. When the lot fell on Jonah, he fessed

"Fear of the LORD *is our lifesaver in deep waters."*—MaryEllen

up. Acknowledging that his God had sent the storm because of him, Jonah bid them to throw him overboard to save themselves. The sailors were afraid if they did, Jonah's God would hold them accountable for killing Jonah. Consequently, they rowed fervently to return to land but their efforts were for naught. The crew prayed to Jonah's God, begging for safety and to not be charged with Jonah's death, after which they promptly tossed Jonah over the rails into the jaws of the angry waters. The sea calmed. Immediately, the men's fear of circumstances converted into a fear of the Lord, for at that moment they realized this God did indeed control the universe. At once, they vowed to worship Him.

In the meantime, God sent a great fish to swallow Jonah. For three days and nights Jonah sloshed around in the creature's belly. This wasn't exactly what Jonah had in mind. (At this point did he question his prophet power?) Finally conceding his predicament, Jonah figured it best to no longer deny the presence of the Lord. Jonah cried out to God, admitting his need for Him and offering a voice of thanksgiving.

God spoke to the fish, which at once upchucked Jonah onto dry ground.

God spoke to Jonah to get up and go to Nineveh to deliver a message. Jonah went. Once in Nineveh—a city so great it took three days to visit it all—Jonah proclaimed that God would overturn Nineveh in forty days. Ninevites believed the news. In fear of impending destruction, the king sent out a decree for a fast and a dress of sackcloth, and urged everyone to pray to the living God and to give up their evil and violent ways.

When Jonah saw God pour compassion and mercy on the repentant and transformed Ninevites, he got mad. In essence, Jonah said, "See, God, what'd I tell you? I delivered your message of doom and now I look foolish because here I am a prophet and it didn't come to pass. I knew all along you'd just forgive our enemy. That's why I didn't want to come here in the first place. Just put me out of my misery. I'm better off dead."

Jonah moped out of the city and sat down to sulk. God supplied a shady vine to comfort him. Not totally ungrateful, Jonah was glad for the plant. As the sun rose the following morning, God sent a worm to gnaw at the greenery. Later in the scorching heat of the day, Jonah about fainted under the withered plant, and made it quite clear to God how he felt about the situation.

God replied, "Do you have a right to be angry about the (withering) vine?"

In contemporary words, Jonah said, "Sure do, angry enough to die right here on the spot."

The Lord would have none of Jonah's self-centeredness and chastised him for having concern for the vine which he had neither tended nor watered, but had had no concern for the lost people of Nineveh.

In short, Jonah had not trusted God with how the end results would affect him. Rather, he feared risking his reputation as a prophet. This type of fear led him into distrust and almost brought about his demise.

On the other hand, the threat of imminent demise brought the Ninevites to a fear of the Lord and into a position of trusting Him for their present and future, where they would no longer fear circumstances.

> *"Fear of the LORD is a fountain of life, turning a man from the snares of death."*
> *—Proverbs 14:27*

FRUITS OF FEARING THE LORD

Because I fear the Lord, I will not be afraid. When I consider the scope of God's power, both for His ability to destroy that which is evil and protect and restore that which honors His name, I am filled with awe ... and trust. His perfect love casts out fear.

> *"The fear of the LORD is the beginning of wisdom; all who follow his precepts have good understanding...."*—Psalm 111:10

- **When We Fear the Lord, We Gain Wisdom**

What a fruit to harvest! How many times have you wished for wisdom? The Bible makes acquiring it sound easy. All that is required is to fear the Lord. It is that simple. Studying God's Word, hiding it in our hearts and following His laws are the stair steps leading to an awesome reverence—fear of the Lord—for our Creator.

> *"Listen, my son, accept what I say, and the years of your life will be many. I guide you in the way of wisdom and lead you along straight paths. When you walk, your steps will not be hampered; when you run, you will not stumble. Hold on to instruction, do not let it go; guard it well, for it is your life."*—Proverbs 4:10-13

79

- **When We Fear the Lord, We Recognize His Sovereignty**

It is a comfort to realize God is in control. Nothing happens outside of His purview. In times of distress or tragedy, it may help you to anchor to the rock of your salvation by simply uttering the words "God knows all about it. He is here with me now, and He still controls the universe and all that is in it."

- **When We Fear the Lord, We Discern How Awesome He Is**

A Creator who designed Niagara Falls, the sun and moon, dragonflies stitching the air, and the miracle of a newborn baby—and cares about us in the midst of orchestrating the planets and stars—is beyond awesome. We catch only a glimpse of this astounding splendor when we revere His reign over all.

- **When We Fear the Lord, We Accept that He has Only Good in Store for Us**

Each time we submit to God's authority and see the results, we acquire another how-everything-in-our-life puzzle piece fits together. What a beautiful picture the end result is when we not only see that God has only good in store for us, but when we embrace the fullness of the scene, we can step into it and rest there.

- **When We Fear the Lord, We Receive His Love**

Respect for our Lord's dominion opens the floodgates of the love God desires to pour into us. We keep this from happening when we want to do things our way. Fearing the Lord is an avenue that leads us directly to that love.

- **When We Fear the Lord, We Return Love to Him**

God revels in our worship of Him. He knows our hearts and sees how our regard for Him and His statutes play out in our daily lives. Don't you just love loving our Lord and Savior?

- **When We Fear the Lord, We Grow in Knowledge**

Knowledge comes first via our mind. So we must store information there as a foundation. God exhorts us to hide His Word in our hearts. Jesus explained the Parable of the Sower as such: "The knowledge of the secrets of the kingdom of heaven has been given to you ... " (Jesus then continues to link knowledge with understanding.)

- **When We Fear the Lord, We Gain Understanding**

" … When anyone hears the message about the kingdom and does not understand it, the evil one comes and snatches away what was sown in his heart. … When trouble or persecution comes because of the word, he quickly falls away. … But the one who received the seed that fell on good soil is the man who hears the word and understands it. He produces a crop, yielding a hundred, sixty or thirty times what was sown." (Matt. 13:1-23)

Our hearts provide fertile soil for the willingness to allow the Word to take root and grow. So, how do we gain understanding? Does it happen immediately? Presto would be nice, but that's not how seeds sprout, blossom, and produce a harvest. Just as seeds need water, sun, and weeding, so does the Word of God. Only by studying Scriptures, adding verses to our memory banks, tilling His Word for daily nourishment for our minds and spirits, do we come to the understanding of the precept God gives us in Ephesians 5:20. Once we acknowledge His call to thank Him for all things … even when trouble and persecution come … and put it into action, then we come into an understanding of how thanking Him even for our travails will produce a bountiful crop.

Just as He promises in Psalm 111:10, when we follow His precepts, we have good understanding. That word … understanding, or at least a play on the word, brings to mind a recent incident.

Standing Under Brings Understanding …

It was still dark when my husband left for work. I awoke to a blanket of white covering our pasture. Looking out the window, I saw our cattle appearing mournfully hungry, so after getting ready for work, I trounced out the door to throw them some hay. When I returned to the house, I grumbled at the door which had locked behind me on my way out.

No problem. I'll just retrieve the hidden key.

Au contraire. The key wasn't there. I searched and searched to no avail.

I was to be at work in less than an hour and the commute took twenty-plus minutes. Not much time to problem solve. Aha! I remembered I had left an upstairs window unlatched, so I trudged off to unearth a fourteen-foot fiberglass stepladder from under a pile of stuff in the garage. After tugging and lugging, I finally had it up beside the house. The first window was locked. So was the second. These were the easy tries, since those windows were accessible from the deck. Now came the challenge. Our house is built on a slope, so the second story windows are waaaay above ground.

By the time I had the ladder positioned below the third window, I was sweating profusely, and even more so when I saw the top rung didn't even come close to the bottom of the windowsill. So, off to dig out the thirty-foot extension ladder. Do you know how heavy and unwieldy those suckers are? Even when my husband puts it up, he has to have my help.

Now I am crying. I look toward the neighbor's house but know an 87-year-old man who can hardly walk will be of no help. The 72-year-old widow on the other side of our property may be of even less use. The fourth window is locked. I tell the Lord, "I can't do this. I need your help."

He reminds me of His commandment to thank Him for all things. Grrrr. All right, because I know there is wisdom in obeying. "Thank you, God, that I am locked out of my house. Thank you that this ladder is impossible to position and raise high enough to reach the window."

The moment I thanked the Lord for my circumstance, the verse "I can do all things through Christ who strengthens me." infused me with strength and hope. So, with a few more grunts and pushes, at last I was able to complete the task.

After climbing to the top rung, I pried the window open. Immediately, I saw the irony in my situation. Here I was *under* an open window *standing* on the ladder ready to crawl into the house. What had brought me here?

Understanding.

Each time we take God at His Word, we have an even better understanding of how keeping His commandments work to our good, even though they don't always make logical sense. Perhaps this is why the Lord exhorts us to lean not unto our own understanding, i.e. use our intellect to fit Scripture into our comprehension.

> *"My son, if you accept my words and store up my commands within you, turning your ear to wisdom and applying your heart to understanding, and if you call out for insight and cry aloud for understanding, and if you look for it as for silver and search for it as for hidden treasure, then you will understand the fear of the* LORD *and find the knowledge of God."*—Proverbs 2:1-5

Isaiah prophesied the Spirit of the LORD would rest upon Jesus, accompanied by the Spirit of wisdom, understanding, counsel, power, knowledge, and the fear of the LORD, in which He will delight. (Isa. 11:2-3) Rarely in our human way of thinking do we equate fear with delight. Yet in a spiritual sense, it is only when we fear the Lord that we will not be afraid—because we recognize that just as God can destroy, He also saves. As Isaiah wrote, "Surely God is my salvation; I will trust and not be afraid." (Isa. 12:2)

I don't know if there is any man who was more aware of God's power than Isaiah. In his writing, he alludes to the overthrow of Sodom and Gomorrah, God's parting of the Red Sea, God's judgment of fire, and Gideon's victory over Midian, among others. In short, the book of Isaiah unveils the full dimensions of our Lord's judgment and salvation. It is only when we grasp the magnitude of God's power—both ways—that we can associate fear with delight.

With this as a starting point for understanding, I trust His will for my life. When I hold on to His instructions, He guides me along my path. Because of this, I grow in wisdom and understanding. I will endure.

Bible Characters who Feared the Lord Rather Than Their Circumstances

Daniel ... kept the commands of the Lord and continued to pray and give thanks to Him. Because of this King Darius threw him into the lions' den. Although surrounded by the hungry beasts, Daniel endured through the night because he feared not the lions but the Lord, trusting wholeheartedly in his God. (Dan. 6)

Shadrach, **Meshach**, and **Abednego** ... also feared the Lord, loving Him without measure and keeping His commands. For this, Nebuchadnezzar threw them into a blazing furnace, seven times hotter than usual. The furnace was so fiery, flames killed the soldiers who escorted the three men to the inferno. Shadrach, Meshach, and Abednego endured the blaze. In fact, not a hair on their heads was scorched, nor was there any odor of fire on them or their clothing! (Dan. 3)

> *"Fear of God translates into no fear of forging through the fire."*—MaryEllen

Indeed, the fear of the Lord is pure and helps all who love Him to endure forever!

"Great peace have they who love your law, and nothing can make them stumble." (Ps. 119:165)

Joseph … If anyone could or should have stumbled, it would have been Joseph. At seventeen, Joseph's jealous brothers intended to kill him, throwing him down a well. Changing their minds, they pulled him out and sold him into slavery for about eight ounces of silver. How frightened Joseph must have been, and how betrayed he must have felt. Did he ever wonder why not even one brother rescued him, or why his father didn't search for him?

In Egypt, Pharaoh's captain of the guard, Potiphar bought Joseph. The Lord prospered Joseph in his master's house. Because Joseph was blessed by God, Potiphar entrusted everything he owned to Joseph's care.

An attractive and well-built young man, Joseph caught the eye of his master's wife, who invited him to her bed. Joseph refused her because Potiphar trusted him and he did not want to sin against God. The woman persisted day after day, but Joseph continued to refuse her advances. One day, when no one was in the house except Joseph attending to his duties, Potiphar's wife grabbed him. As he pulled away and ran, his cloak remained in her hand. She later showed it to Potiphar, crying out that Joseph had tried to take advantage of her.

Thrown into prison for something he hadn't done, Joseph had every reason to give up on God. He could have wailed, "I kept your commands and what did I get for it? Why should I remain faithful to you?" And yet he didn't stumble. Joseph continued in his faith and love for God.

The Lord was with Joseph in prison and gave him the warden's favor. Joseph was once again in a management position. I'm afraid if I were Joseph I would have been tempted to complain, "Lord, what good does it do to have the trust of those in charge when I'm still not a free man?"

When Joseph was thirty years old, Pharaoh had a dream. The Pharaoh's cupbearer suddenly remembered Joseph had correctly interpreted his dream when he was in prison, so he shared this with the king. Pharaoh summoned Joseph, who gave credit to God for the interpretation that revealed seven years of prosperity in the land would be followed by seven years of famine. Joseph advised Pharaoh to store up grain. Because of his wise counsel, Joseph was put in charge of all Egypt, second in power only to the king.

Just as predicted, in time, famine arrived throughout the world. Joseph's brothers traveled to Egypt to purchase grain and appeared before Joseph. They didn't recognize him, and Joseph, throwing them into jail, didn't reveal himself as their brother. On the third day he said to them, "Do this (leave one brother in prison, but return with the youngest brother) and you will live, for I fear God."

Finally, Joseph, now thirty-nine years old, revealed his identity and told them it was God who sent him to Egypt to preserve a remnant (of Israel) on earth and to deliver them from famine. (Gen. 37-42)

It may be hard for us to see in the midst of difficult times that God is leading us along straight paths. Could Joseph, who had spent over half of his life separated from his family and the land of his youth, have seen his journey as a straight path? Perhaps looking down from God's view, or looking back from a historical observation point, we might be able to more clearly see the progression of Joseph's pilgrimage.

Joseph's Journey:

Thrown down a well by his brothers
⇩
Sold to slave traders
⇩
Potiphar's servant
⇩
Falsely accused by Potiphar's wife
⇩
Imprisoned for several years
⇩
Pharaoh's overseer of all Egypt
⇩
Preserves Israel's lineage

Fearing God had helped Joseph not to stumble. Additionally, it helped him not only to endure for a season of captivity but had made it possible for Israel to literally endure forever!

Until we get to "the rest of the story," it certainly doesn't seem like a straight path. You, too, will endure your season of tribulations because God's commands lead the way, thereby incinerating briars and snares, illuminating potholes, eliminating obstructions, and exterminating Satan's ruses so you will not stumble. When we understand that God has only good in store for us, we have the courage to stand firm in Him and meet whatever comes into our path.

"Who is wise? He will realize these things. Who is discerning? He will understand them. The ways of the LORD are right; the righteous walk in them, but the rebellious stumble in them."—Hosea 14:9

P.S.

With the Lord's help, after getting the thirty-foot ladder into place and climbing into the second-story window, I rushed downstairs. Hurrying out the door, I noticed the extra key on the countertop. When I returned home from work that evening, I discovered my husband had also locked himself out early in the morning when he left for work but had to come back in for something. He didn't want to wake me, so had retrieved the hidden key to let himself in and had left it in the kitchen for me. *Thank you, Lord, for such a thoughtful husband.*

౸

Invitation to Personal Prayer

Thank you, Lord, for helping me recognize that when I fear my circumstances, I do not trust that you are working for my good. But when I accept and reverence your control, i.e. fear of the Lord, I can trust in you.

Memory Verse

"The fear of the LORD is pure, enduring forever."
Psalm 19:9

9

Trusting in God in Fear of the Intruder

"Fear of man will prove to be a snare, but whoever trusts in
the LORD is kept safe."
Proverbs 29:25

I have written about having been burglarized five times. Please allow me to fill
in some blanks.

The first time they didn't get much, only an item or two from our barn. The
second time, only two weeks later while our old ranch house was vacant and in
the midst of remodeling, they stole contractor's tools and equipment worth
several thousand dollars. The third time, I was left incredulous. We had just purchased bathroom articles ... a sink and cabinet, frosted glass medicine cabinet,
toilets, etc., all in boxes awaiting a next-day installation. When we arrived the
following morning, all was gone. Except the toilets.

Once we moved in, I finally gained a sense of security. Surely no one would
break in with us living there. At least I hoped not, especially since my husband
had been promoted to foreman and transferred to swing shift, which left me
home alone until he returned around midnight.

My sense of security was short-lived. As I settled down to read, something like a magnet drew my gaze to a smudge beneath the window to my side. Freshly painted walls emphasized a trail of dirt. Alarm ricocheted throughout my body. I froze, my gaze now riveted on something even more chilling. Fingerprints on the outside of the windowpane formed a pattern in an upward streak, as if someone had pushed up the window.

Immediately, the scene played out in my head. *The window opening. A leg thrust inside. His dirty shoe sliding down the wall.* A dusty footprint on our new carpet confirmed the scenario.

Fear and anxiety kicked in, making it difficult for me to remain calm. However, determined not to cave in to wild imaginings, I decided to check one more thing outside. Coming around the house, I skidded to a halt. A flattened molehill beneath the window revealed footprints.

I frantically searched inside for evidence of anything missing. But everything seemed in order. *Why would someone break in and not take anything? Was he casing the house? Was he coming back to hurt me? Did he know I was home alone?*

Eventually, I went to bed but couldn't sleep. The phone rang. It was my husband; he had to work overtime and wouldn't be home until two a.m. I didn't mention what I'd seen because he often accuses me of overreacting. I would wait to show him the evidence, show him I was not making a mountain out of a molehill.

After hanging up the receiver, my mind took on a life of its own. *Sure the intruder would pick that window because that's the only side of the house without a motion sensor. Maybe I scared him off when I came home from work. Or . . . what if he's hiding in the attic? Or in the closet? What was that sound?* Each thought flashed in panoramic cinemascope.

> *"He fulfills the desires of those who fear him; he hears their cry and saves them."*
> —*Psalm 145:19*

With my heart pounding and my mouth dry, I prayed, "Lord protect me."

At once, a verse came to mind. *"My perfect love casts out all fear."*

A mental acrostic of FEAR emerged.

Fiction

Effectively

Acting

Real

What was fictional about what I'd seen? I hadn't imagined the finger smudges, dirt trail, or footprints. They were as real as the glass and carpet on which they'd been planted. Of this I had knowledge, so obviously the error had to be in my understanding.

Help me, Lord.

For such as this very moment God has had me store His Word in my heart. Surely, if ever I needed a weapon, it was now. Taking up the Sword of the Spirit, I recited verses as the Lord brought them to mind.

"He will cover you with his feathers, and under his wings you will find refuge; his faithfulness will be your shield and rampart. You will not fear the terror of night ...." (Ps. 91:4-5)

"If you make the Most High your dwelling—even the LORD, who is my refuge—then no harm will befall you, no disaster will come near your tent." (Ps. 91:9-10)

More Scriptures flowed, blanketing me with protection and peace. Then a message whispered into my thoughts, *Bob locked himself out of the house today. He came in through the window.*

> *The LORD confides in those who fear him; he makes his covenant known to them."—Psalm 25:14*

Ah, for the reassurance of truth and understanding.

The next morning I commented to my husband about him locking himself out of the house.

He seemed surprised. "How did you know?"

I smiled and realized the only intruder had been the spirit of fear.

How do I know it was a spirit? 2 Timothy 1:7 identifies it as such: "For God hath not given us a spirit of fear, but of power, of love, and of a sound mind." (*KJV*) Paul recognized this same spirit, and in writing to the people of the church at Rome firmly stated, "For you did not receive a spirit that makes you a slave again to fear, but you received the Spirit of sonship." (Rom. 8:15)

Likewise, people of the Gerasenes region were also victims of this spirit from Satan. On the eastern shore of the Sea of Galilee, a demon-possessed man fell at Jesus' feet as he stepped out of a boat. The tormented man begged Jesus not to torture him because Jesus had commanded the evil spirit to depart from him.

More demons revealed themselves and pleaded with Jesus not to order them into the Abyss, but to send them into a nearby herd of pigs. Upon seeing the pigs then rush into the lake, Looky-Lous along the bank immediately spread the word and everyone in the region was overcome with fear and asked Jesus to leave. (Mk. 5:11-17)

> " *... but whoever listens to me will live in safety and be at ease, without fear of harm."*
> —*Proverbs 1:33*

Is it possible a spirit of fear had escaped the drowned pigs and taken up residence in the people round about? The spirit of fear is sent from the enemy. Satan is an accuser, a liar, a thief. He wants to steal our peace and get our eyes off Jesus and onto worldly circumstances so he can batter us about. But whether it is Satan or our own minds that conjure up fictional scenarios, or twist the truth, the result remains the same. When we entertain thoughts contrary to God's Word, we end up in worry and fear. And fear torments us. So the choice is ours. We can run in the path of God's commands out of fear (reverence) for Him, or we can run in the path of fear of our circumstances—or fear of man. The former is a run propelled by freedom. The latter is a run right into the crosshairs of Satan's aim to take us down.

༄

Invitation to Personal Reflection

What do you fear?

1. _____
2. _____
3. _____
4. _____
5. _____

Invitation to Personal Prayer

Lord, I love you but I confess these are the things of which I am afraid. I realize my fear is of the enemy and I know it is a result of not fully understanding and taking you at your Word. I want to be made perfect in love. Please help me hide the following verses in my heart that I may use them as the Sword of the Spirit to fend off fear, that I may be freed from each of the above which I have placed in your caring hands.

Memory Verses

"There is no fear in love; but perfect love casteth out fear; because fear hath torment. He that feareth is not made perfect in love."
I John 4:18 (*KJV*)

"The LORD is with me; I will not be afraid; What can man do to me?"
Psalm 118:6

"For I am the LORD your God who takes hold of your right hand and says to you, Do not fear; I will help you."
Isaiah 41:13

～10～

Warning! Troubles & Great Rewards Ahead

"I have told you these things, so that in me you may have peace. In this world you will have trouble. But take heart! I have overcome the world."
John 16:33

God clearly warns us that we will have trouble. None is exempt from this fact. It's just that troubles vary in size and severity. Troubles one day may include minor irritations but the next day might bring about life-changing tragedy.

A minor irritation visited our house as I was writing this chapter. Notifications came from both house insurance and car insurance companies that our premiums were going up because our credit report showed an excess of charge cards.

Their letters read:

"Your consumer reporting agency, Trans Union, indicated too many consumer finance company accounts. Research shows that consumers with consumer finance company loans appearing on their credit report represent higher insurance loss risk than those with no consumer finance company loans."

As far as I knew, I had only one credit card for emergency use, which I faithfully pay off monthly. After requesting a credit report, I was surprised to read

Trans Union reported me with six charge accounts. Looking more closely, I saw I had not used five of them for between six and sixteen years. In the past, we had purchased furniture or carpet on delayed payment deals. Of course, I had always paid them off within the allotted time frame. Nonetheless the accounts glared from the page.

> *"The longer we dwell on our misfortunes, the greater is their power to harm us."—Voltaire*

Something else jumped out at me. An attempt to save 15%, or some such bargain, now cost more than I'd saved. Over the years, I'd filled out credit applications at JC Penny, the GAP, etc. to get those precious few dollars' savings during sales promotions. Although I'd never used those credit cards after the initial purchases, they remained on my credit report as active charge accounts.

Clenching my teeth, I thanked God for this minor trouble. Immediately, I realized rising insurance rates were a signal to clean up my credit report.

This contemporary kind of trouble perhaps rates as pesky as niggling deer flies in Biblical times. As a shepherd, David no doubt anointed sheep heads with oil to keep deer flies from pestering them. When David wrote, "You anoint my head with oil." he likely was thinking about how faithful God was to keep daily nuisances from bugging him.

Little troubles we expect. They pale in comparison to the tragedies we do not see coming, as in Paddy's life ....

Paddy's Story

I had just finished a public reading at a literary event, Northwest Voices, when a smiling lady approached and expressed appreciation for my story. After Paddy introduced herself to me, we discussed our mutual love of writing. A few months later, I called to ask if she would like to join my writing critique group. Elated at the invitation, she accepted. Sadly, circumstances prevented her from joining us.

Two-and-a-half years later, we met for an interview. Following are excerpts from our conversation.

Paddy, how would you like to begin your story?

"It was a moment in time that totally altered every member of our family's life.

"Shortly after our twentieth wedding anniversary, my husband was returning from his dad's after midnight. He must have been momentarily inattentive, or he saw a deer or something, but he swerved off the road. His van flipped over and over, then back up on its wheels about fifty-two feet away. He suffered a traumatic brain injury and was in a coma for five months. Now, he has a hard time eating by mouth, so he's got a tummy tube and he can't get out of bed without a Hoyer lift. His hearing and sight work. He can smile and he does that often.

"Rick and I were best friends, humanly—because of course Jesus is our very best friend. He was my husband, my business partner, and my brother in the Lord, so we had those four different levels of our relationship, and I feel as though I've lost …" (Paddy takes a moment to compose herself.)

"He's not able to participate in our plumbing business anymore. It's really hard. Physically he's not able to do much at all, but emotionally he seems to have deepened; his emotions are very appropriate to the situation. He is quick to cry at a sad moment. He smiles and laughs any time of day. If anyone walks into the room, he greets them with a big smile. Two weeks ago he finally said his first sentence.

"He said, 'I lov … y … I lov … y…'

"I said, 'Are you talking?'

"He said, 'I lov … y…'

"Are you saying 'I love you?'

"He pointed and nodded.

"I said, 'Say it again.' And he did. I said, 'Thank you so much. I lost a bet, though. I thought when you finally spoke you would say, 'I'm hungry. Give me a steak. Or, I'm tired.' It made me cry right then. He's always given me every bit of his paycheck, everything he's ever had. Since his accident, he's totally given me everything he has to give. Without saying a word, because he can't speak, he gets across all kinds of important concepts. Like if you phrase a question and ask for a yes or no, he says yes and no with his fingers. One finger for yes, two for no.

When I mentioned I was basing my book on Ephesians 5:20 and asked if you have ever applied it to the 24-hour care of your husband, what was your reaction?

"I had to look it up. I didn't know the Scripture by heart. But I love the Word of God. Every bit I've tested personally has always proven true. A day or two prior to this interview, I had been getting the same concept from the Lord—that if I would just stop praying and just praise Him and thank Him for all of it that I'd see the results eventually.

"Two weeks after I started praising the Lord and thanking Him for everything, Rick was able to say 'I love you.' If Rick never says anything else, that's enough." (Paddy giggles.)

Did you ever have any anger that God would ask you to thank Him for having to care for a quadriplegic husband?

"Instead of remembering all the good things Rick had done, I started to think of all the mistakes he'd made which were not that many, but there were some. The anger about my situation as a result of Rick's accident was basically that I was left handling 100% of everything that needed to be done. It took about two years for that to catch up to me. We lost our plumbing business. We gave up our house to move into an apartment. I was feeling trapped by the situation. I wanted to go forward with my life but I couldn't because Rick is still here even though he can't do any of the things he used to do as a husband. I want to have a fulfilling marriage." (Paddy stops, reflects.)

"Actually, Rick is my second husband.

"For the last three years of my first marriage, I was a Christian. My then-husband kept saying, 'You're not the girl I married,' which meant I wouldn't go to bars with him. When he left me and a week later married a woman I didn't know, I was devastated.

"I had four kids under the age of ten to raise by myself. I needed something to cheer me up—something more than a latte. So, I put ten dollars down on a wedding gown. I didn't have a groom in mind but maybe someone would want me someday." (Paddy laughs.)

"Two years later, I paid off the dress. By then, with it hanging in the closet, I surrendered the whole idea of marriage. I said to God, 'You have taken great care of me and the kids and if you never want me to get married again, that's okay I'll just be *your* bride.' Within a week, I got four marriage proposals. Monday. Tuesday. Wednesday. Thursday. Four! They were just acquaintances—a neighbor, a brother of a friend, etc. I wasn't in love with any of them. One guy begged me to wear his ring overnight and just think about marrying him. I knew I wasn't going to. By Friday, though, I was kind of in a marrying mood. I said, 'Lord, are you trying to tell me it's okay to get married again?'

"Friday, I met Ricky. His car was broken down, and he was hitchhiking near a smelly dairy farm. I couldn't even stand driving past; I'd hate to have to stand by it. I prayed, 'Lord, is it safe to pick him up?'

"I heard the Lord laugh and say, 'Yes.'

"So, I picked Rick up and took him to the top of the hill. I asked if he knew the Lord. He said, 'I don't do church. The last girlfriend I had, I lost because I don't go to church. I'm open but I'm a backslider.' I liked his honesty.

"He said, 'You don't want anything to do with me. I'm a mess.'

"I said, 'Oh, an honest guy!'

"We talked about where I was with the Lord. I invited him to church. We went to Casey Treat's church in Seattle. At the altar call Rick stood up, and I thought, *he's going to leave.* But he ran forward and knelt down. He told me that's what he needed—Jesus. He accepted the Lord that day.

"From then on, he's had his own amazing journey with the Lord. This accident is part of it. I knew when it happened it was between him and God. God allowed it. He's working on Rick. And me."

What blessings has God shown you as a reward for your faithfulness to thank Him for this?

"I've had to abandon some of my dreams and goals that Rick and I had, but now I have bigger ones. I'm in a very exciting stage in life because I've put Rick in God's hands. I know God's working everything for good. I just don't know His timeline. I feel overwhelmed by how blessed I feel. It's a good space.

"I've been given hope that if Rick doesn't recover in this life, there's something more later. I have freedom and am totally at peace."

What words of encouragement would you give to other women facing tragedies?

"Trust that God works to the good for everyone concerned in your situation. If you patiently ride out the storm—the tragedy you have to deal with—there is always something that more than compensates afterward."

༄

Several weeks after our interview, Paddy emailed me with great news. Rick is now able to stand in his standing frame and, with help, is making progress toward taking a few steps at a time. I do not have to wonder at this miracle. I am convinced that when Paddy began thanking God for her and Rick's circumstances it was not by chance that after two-and-a-half years of immobility, Rick is standing and will soon be walking. Even if only in baby steps at first.

"Birds sing after a storm; why shouldn't people feel as free to delight in whatever remains to them?"
—*Rose Fitzgerald Kennedy*

The other good news is that Rick has a new communication device, similar to an Etch-a-Sketch in size and shape but more like a laptop computer in functionality. Rick touches a picture on the screen and the computer says whatever it's programmed to say, thus allowing Rick to verbalize his thoughts for the first time since February 22, 2003.

Paddy says she is going to have fun with this. Tongue in cheek, she shares some of the entries she will program on at least one screen of Rick's new toy; the screen she calls "Mr. Wonderful."

- Yes, Dear.
- Whatever you say, Sweetheart.
- Certainly. How soon would you like that done?
- Where would you like to shop next?
- I'll be happy to fold the laundry.
- Have you lost weight?
- Can I massage your shoulders?
- The dishes can wait. Come watch this Chick Flick with me.
- Here's the remote.

෨

What a testimony to Paddy's character that she is able to embrace reality and have fun with it. Paddy is, indeed, able to take hold of the great reward that comes from loving and trusting the Lord. She has found that she doesn't have to understand God's plan to accept and trust it.

John 16:33 mentions peace and trouble. Paddy has both. With Jesus as her Lord and Savior, her troubles are temporary, her peace permanent.

It is people like Paddy, whose hearts are fully committed to God, who position themselves in the only perfect place—in the Lord's hands. Asa, King of Judah, also shared this perfect place with Paddy, even if a few years earlier—910-869 B.C.

King Asa

For the first ten years of his reign, Asa relied wholly on the Lord God. He tore down idols and altars of foreign gods. Asa led his countrymen to seek God and to obey His statutes. During this decade, no other armies came against Asa, for the Lord gave him rest. After Asa built up towns and prospered, the Cushites attacked. King Asa maintained his steadfastness in God, calling out, "'LORD, there is no one like you to help the powerless against the mighty.'" (2 Chron. 14:11) Ever faithful, God struck down the Cushites, and gave Asa rest for many more years.

However, in Asa's thirty-sixth year of reign, the King of Israel came against Judah. Asa withdrew silver and gold from the temple of God and sent it to the King of Aram, requesting that the two of them form a pact. He asked the King of Aram to break his treaty with the King of Israel so Israel would withdraw from Judah. The ploy worked … sort of.

Sort of, in that while the Israeli army abandoned its invasion, King Asa now had another problem.

A seer came to Asa and pointed out how foolish Asa had been to rely on man rather than on God. The seer cited previous instances of Asa's defeats of mighty Cushite and Libyan armies when Asa had relied upon the Lord.

Asa became angry and threw the seer into prison. Subsequently, Asa had another problem—a diseased foot. Despite the severity of this illness, Asa did not seek the Lord, but relied *solely* on help from physicians. A year later, Asa died.

I hope this story from 2 Chronicles is as enlightening to you as it is to me. It is full of promises and clearly illustrates how wise it is to put our faith in God in the midst of the storm. Did you know the Lord is constantly on the lookout for those to whom He can give strength?

"For the eyes of the LORD range throughout the earth to strengthen those whose hearts are fully committed to him." (2 Chron. 16:9)

Turning Deerflies & Disaster into Opportunities

"Be very careful, then, how you live—not as unwise but as wise, making the most of every opportunity, because the days are evil."—Ephesians 5:15

Big or small, pests or mammoth troubles, the Lord is with us through them all. Daily deerflies and disasters as significant as Paddy's and King Asa's fit into God's promise of trouble. Both are gifts. For we know that when trouble comes, it doesn't mean God has deserted us, or that He is powerless. Instead, it is an opportunity for us to experience His peace and the power of The One Who has overcome the world.

> *"Trouble is only opportunity in work clothes."*—Henry J. Kaiser

His peace fills us and guards our hearts and minds. This sentry of peace keeps anxiety at bay and allows us to rejoice as we climb to even greater heights. When we cross that threshold of thanksgiving—which is a true demonstration of our reliance upon and trust in God—we open the door to peace that goes beyond all understanding.

Thanksgiving—a Great Way to Let God Help

Giving thanks to the Lord turns us back to Him and positions us to let Him help us. Consider what it cost King Asa when he didn't let God help him.

ᕲᕲ

Invitation to Personal Reflection

What has it cost you when you didn't let God help?

* Spiritually …

- Mentally ...

- Emotionally ...

- Tangibly ...

When you totally relied upon God, what were the results?

- Spiritually ...

- Mentally ...

- Emotionally ...

- Tangibly ...

I encourage you to turn your deerflies—those things bugging you—and your disasters into opportunities. You will be amazed at the peace, revelations, and release you experience in the process.

((## Invitation to Personal Prayer   ))

Lord, I admit I have groused about _____.
Now I am seizing this situation as an opportunity to apply the precept of thanksgiving. Thank you for _____.

Okay, Lord, it was easier to start with the deerflies in my life. Thanking you for _____ is much harder. It is more difficult to comprehend how a disaster is an opportunity. Nonetheless, I am stepping out in faith. If Paddy can thank you for her devastating circumstances, I can do so as well. Thank you that _____ happened in my life. I am trusting you for the peace in it all, for the revelation of your perspective, and for release from my pain and torment. God, even though I may never be thankful for this tragedy in my life, I give you thanks for it, knowing you have not abandoned me, but that you have great things in store for me.

((## Memory Verse   ))

"Rejoice in the Lord always. I will say it again: Rejoice! . . . The Lord is near. Do not be anxious about anything, but in everything, by prayer and petition, with thanksgiving, present your requests to God. And the peace of God, which transcends all understanding, will guard your hearts and your minds in Christ Jesus."
Philippians 4:4-7

~11~

10 Must-Do's When Bad Things Happen

"Let the word of Christ richly dwell within you, with all
wisdom teaching and admonishing one another with psalms
and hymns and spiritual songs, singing with thankfulness in
your hearts to God."
Colossians 3:16 (New American Standard Bible)

Vicky returned home to discover her house had been broken into and ransacked. Rob lost his job of twenty years; his bills mount. Beth's teenager wrecked her car and now lies in the hospital, a breath away from never breathing again.

In my counseling practice, I have met people who experienced such terrible misfortunes. May none of these situations ever happen to you. But if tragedy does storm into your life like the intruder breaking through Vicky's door, you can be armed and ready for the onslaught.

How? By making healthy choices.

Unfortunately, in a crisis the norm is to resort to detrimental behaviors—taking comfort in junk food, withdrawing, anesthetizing with wine or soap operas. Rather than helping you cope, these actions usher in depression, or at best, render you ineffective in taking care of business.

The key to confronting bad things, rather than becoming victim to them, is to be prepared. If you wait until a tragedy occurs, you will find it almost impossible to think clearly. Being ready will help you navigate tumultuous waters—physically, mentally, emotionally, and spiritually. Here is a list of 10 must-do-things that, when carried out, will buoy your whole self.

1. Regular Routine

As much as possible, keep to routine. Rob didn't. Instead, unemployed, he rose around noon, switched on TV and watched game shows all day wishing he could be the one fortunate enough to win that million dollars. From there, he spiraled downward.

The sameness and cadence of a regular routine helps you maintain normalcy in abnormal circumstances. If you lose your source of income, it is critical to stick to your usual reading of the newspaper over breakfast, showering before bedtime, or whatever you have always done outside of your employment.

Rise each morning as previously; but now instead of heading out the door to work, spend the next eight hours filling out applications, attending job search workshops, networking, etc.

Conversely, if, as Beth does, you now face a hectic schedule because of trips to the hospital to be with your loved one while still holding down a job, chauffeuring children to school and sports, cooking, cleaning, laundry, and such, then ask yourself: *What can I let go of and still retain routine and sanity?* Prioritize within your daily schedule.

2. Exercise & Fresh Air

Hopefully, exercise and fresh air are a customary part of your day. If not, add this dynamic combination to your schedule. Exercising outdoors—even in inclement weather—will prove to be the premium in your gas tank, the extra boost your body and soul need. You may resist, arguing, "How can I cram anything more into my day?"

The real question is, "How much time do you spend in front of the television or computer?" Investing a mere quarter of an hour walking briskly around the block will reap healthy dividends: focused thoughts, clearer lungs, de-stressed muscles, and an invigorated body. Know this for certain: You will notice a wonderful difference in your stamina, energy, and mood.

3. Eat Healthy Foods & Drink Lots of Water

You know what would happen if you put sugar in your car's gas tank before driving up a mountain. Yet you may disregard the special fuel your body requires to function at optimum level. Isn't it great that God made fruits, vegetables, fish, whole grains, and water less expensive than fast-food grease patties, ho-hum snacks, or crispy-crumby donuts? To boot, natural foods don't leave a coat of lard on the tongue or drop a gut bomb!

You dispute, "It's easier to grab a candy bar."

Since you are already in the grocery store, why not cruise by the vegetable aisle where trimmed and bagged veggie snacks await you?

"I don't have time to grocery shop," you counter. "It's quicker to drive through fast food."

If quick is what you want, then order a salad. And a free, large cup of water.

Water won't deteriorate your bones as does the phosphoric acid in soda pop. To the contrary, H_2O balances your body's electrolytes—a great help against stress. Why wouldn't you want your body operating on all cylinders so it can efficiently and effectively transport you through rocky terrain?

4. Rest

Refresh your body with sleep. Without it, your thoughts jumble, muscles fumble, and emotions grumble. But what if all you desire is sleep? For a day or so, maybe this is what your body requires. However, more downtime than that speaks of a depressed state, and you may need a friend or family member to come alongside to help you emerge from this abyss. Make preparations even now. Propose to a friend or family member: "If ever either of us can't get out of bed, would you agree with me to do whatever it takes to rescue the other from the blanket of despondency?"

What if you have difficulty sleeping? Then go to bed at the usual time. Set your alarm as customary. Use your bed for rest. If you have a television in your bedroom, remove it. An hour or two prior to lying down, drink a glass of milk, eat a light snack of anything with tryptophan—a natural sleep inducer—such as nuts or seeds, turkey, bananas, or any dairy product. Additionally, tryptophan is proven to help reduce anxiety and elevate mood.

Pave the path to slumber with relaxing music. Direct your thoughts to pleasant things. Create a mental file now: hummingbirds dangling mid-air, the moon reflecting off a lake at midnight, the sweet fragrance of springtime lilacs, your baby's first laugh.

5. Talk it Out

As a Counselor, I witness firsthand the advantages of talking things out. When you stifle emotions and refuse to release your whirlwind of thoughts, they hold you hostage to your circumstances. Find someone you trust to talk to, someone who will keep things confidential, who is understanding, and non-judgmental. (S)he doesn't have to have all the answers, just a caring and listening ear.

Letting emotions out, such as worry and dread, is like releasing air from an over-inflated balloon before it bursts.

6. Keep in Sight that which is Good

When you are in the midst of tragedy, you can focus on the murk and mire of it all or you can set your sights on the good and right in your life. Make an inventory now. Add to it. What will you write? *I have a Lord who loves me. I have shelter and ample food. I have a good reputation. I am able to walk wherever I want to go. I am told I have an encouraging smile. My children love me. I do not want for clothes.* Record good things in your life.

Then when bad things happen, you will have your list as a reminder; it will tug your focus away from the bad.

7. Escape Momentarily

Escape can be good or bad. Escape into alcohol or drugs only makes a bad situation worse. However, momentary flights from reality such as drifting away in a hot bath, fading into the scene of an uplifting movie, retreating into an engaging book, or ebbing away to the beach, these things revive the body and soul, and fortify one's resolve and strength to push through bad times.

8. Bathe in Music

Surround sound—ahh, the bliss of inspiring, encouraging music. You know just what soars your spirit. As well, you know which songs shove you toward self-pity. Choose music that fits you with wings to lift and carry you through the darkness. Have these CD's at the ready, perched on your desk or shelf, or better yet already loaded in your car's player, standing by for the moment of need. One tiny push of the button will make a big difference in your day.

9. Arm Yourself with Scripture

Philippians 4:13 is a fantastic friend, a reminder of truth—*I can do all things through Christ who gives me strength.* Use it, whether you locked your keys in the car, or you are lying in the hospital in excruciating pain. This Scripture will extract you from the talons of despair.

Memorizing verses in advance will provide you with an arsenal from which to draw when you need a weapon to pierce the enemy of hopelessness. Another awesome arrow for your quiver is Jeremiah 29:11: *"'For I know the plans I have for you,' declares the LORD, 'plans to prosper you and not to harm you, plans to give you hope and a future . . . .'"* Write encouraging verses on sticky notes, index cards, or bookmarks. Keep them handy in your purse, in your car, on the bathroom mirror.

10. Dwell with God

There is prayer, which goes: "Dear, God, please help me through this. Amen." And then there is *prayer*—hopping into the Lord's lap, drinking in the essence of His presence.

How do you do this?

Connect with Him through Worship and Praise.

As suggested in #8 Must-Do, music is one means of transportation into the Holy of Holies. Maybe you worship best by quietly singing *In the Garden*. Perhaps your favorite Bill Gaither CD or tape ministers to you. Or is it Michael W. Smith who lifts you to that place of worship and praise?

And as suggested in #9 Must-Do, another way to dwell with our Lord is through immersion in His Word. This will position you in the embrace of the Lord of Lords and King of Kings. If you are too far down in the mollygrubs to pick up the Bible, ask that special friend to read aloud to you.

And as you may have guessed by now, thanking our Heavenly Father will transport you into His presence. *Thank you, Lord, for this opportunity to draw nearer to you. Thank you that I can come to you any hour of the day or night, and that you always have time for me. Thank you that you know all about my situation and are carrying me through it. Thank you for the peace that passes all understanding of my circumstances.*

༄

Bad things *will* invade your life; but if you arm yourself with these Must-Do's, you will be a step ahead of the tragedy, and the intruder will not be able to steal you away from a much better place to be, the place of peace.

༄

⟨ **Invitation to Personal Reflection** ⟩

What are healthy changes you want to make in your lifestyle that will prepare you for meeting a crisis with more stamina? For example, build a fifteen-minute walk into your lunch break, park at the outer edge of your grocery store's lot, and prepare fresh vegetables for snacks and keep them available in the fridge.

1. _____
2. _____
3. _____
4. _____
5. _____

⟨ **Invitation to Personal Prayer** ⟩

Lord Jesus, I desire to be as spiritually, physically, emotionally, and
mentally healthy as possible. Please help me see doable things that
will strengthen me. Thank you for the encouragement to make these a
habit. Amen.

⟨ **Memory Verse** ⟩

"For the LORD watches over the way of the righteous ..."
Psalm 1:6

∾ 12 ∾

Without Pain Where Would We Be?

"It was good for me to be afflicted so that I might learn
your decrees."
Psalm 119:71

"Character cannot be developed in ease and quiet. Only
through experience of trial and suffering can the soul be
strengthened, ambition inspired, and success achieved."
Helen Keller

The Foundation Laid

I began this book telling of the Women's Retreat and how, after laying the foundation, I witnessed ladies thanking God for everything in their lives—from death to abuse to illness, and more. Having entered the little country church that frosty spring morning, I was apprehensive on the one hand, yet on the other trusting God to carry the women to a place of freedom. He did it by building a firm foundation upon which they could stand. It was a foundation comprised of revelations and promises. Revelations and promises that unveiled wisdom, joy, light, sweetness, and great reward that were theirs for the taking. By grasping His commands—a light in their hands—they could step onto the path to freedom. In short, they were prepared to embrace Ephesians 5:20, to thank God for ALL THINGS. These sisters in Christ realized God was not asking them to *be* thankful but to simply, out of faith and trust, *give* Him thanks.

Another Sister in the Lord—Corrie ten Boom

In *The Hiding Place*[4], Corrie ten Boom tells of her and her sister Betsie's suffering in Hitler's concentration camps. Each night as they returned to their bunks—straw-covered platforms where many women crowded together to "sleep"—they experienced exasperating flea bites and ceaseless itching. Betsie reminded Corrie of a Bible verse they had read that morning—to give thanks in all circumstances. Together, they began thanking God for the Bible they were able to smuggle into the prison, and for not having been separated from each other. But when Betsie thanked God for the little bloodsuckers, Corrie uttered that even the Lord couldn't make her grateful for the infestation. Undaunted, Betsie repeated the Lord's admonishment to give thanks in ALL circumstances. Corrie capitulated and thanked God for the vermin, although she still wasn't convinced Betsie was right in this case.

It was only later that Corrie realized how the fleas had played a vital part in God's work. Because of the pest invasion, guards would not step foot in Barracks 28. Thus, Betsie and Corrie were able to have Bible studies there and minister to fellow prisoners.

Corrie ten Boom is a woman after my own heart. I have grumbled many times about thanking God for things for which I can see no earthly reason to thank Him. Sometimes it takes a couple of years for me to get the "wisdom," "joy," "revival of my soul," and "reward" from being obedient.

What Does a No-Bull-Tail Tale Have to do with an International Presentation?

As I write this, my mind somersaults back to Joseph and his journey, and how the series of events in his life turned out to be the straight path God hewed in order to save a remnant of Israel. My upcoming tale isn't as lofty or as dreadful as Joseph's slavery, or Corrie ten Boom's incarceration, but it's my story and

---

4 Ten Boom, Corrie, *The Hiding Place* (New York: Bantam Books, 1974), 198.

I'm sticking to it. It doesn't involve fleas but another of God's creatures. Would I ever have thought I'd be giving thanks for a three-hundred pound steer pinning me to the ground?

It all started with my bright idea of speaking internationally. When it was time to pull my head out of the clouds, (please excuse the cliché, but I *do* live in western Washington state) and start planning, I hopped on the Internet to research exotic venues.

Finding an upcoming conference in Mexico, I immediately shot off my biography and proposal for a presentation on "The Healing Power of Laughter & Play." While I waited for the acceptance, I imagined lounging under palm trees, sifting white sand between my fingers, and soaking up tropical sun, only forcing myself back to the reality of rain long enough to check my mailbox and email.

Even though I had set my hopes high, I was astounded when I received an enthusiastic, "Yes! We want you; you're a perfect fit for our theme."

At once, I began planning a new wardrobe befitting of paradise. All was well until eight weeks before the conference date when I received the agenda. I was scheduled to deliver the opening address on the first morning. On the second day I was listed as presenting a different message.

Hey, wait just a cotton-picking minute, I thought. *I didn't tell her I wanted to speak on* that.

When I'd submitted my bio, I'd included a list of previous Keynote Addresses, one of which was "Giving Thanks for ALL Things." Please don't get me wrong. I love speaking on this topic ... to Christians. But I knew nothing about these ladies. What if they weren't Bible-believers? Audiences heretofore had never had trouble with my "Laughter and Play" presentation—based on Proverbs 17:22 (a merry heart being good medicine)—but "Giving Thanks" required conference attendees to at least be Christ-centered.

"God, how can I tell these women to give thanks for ALL things without bringing you and Scriptures into the message?" I moaned.

"You can't."

It was clear the "I *can't*" didn't mean I *couldn't* deliver the message. Do you ever cringe when God counts on you to do something out of your comfort zone?

In the following weeks, just as I had done with the country church Women's Retreat, I spent a lot of time in prayer. God was giving me a second chance to get it right—to trust Him from the start without question or apprehension. How many times would it take me to pass the test?

That's when *it* happened.

111

"Mary, we're missing a calf. Can you help me look for it?" my husband stated more than asked.

He went one way in our pasture. I went another. Picking my way through waist-high ferns and finagling around blackberry brambles, I came to a three-foot drop-off. I wrapped my right arm around an alder tree to ease down the muddy embankment. My feet went out from underneath me. My arm wrenched behind my head.

So much for finding the calf.

With a torn deltoid muscle, I couldn't raise my right arm—that day, nor the next, nor the next, nor … "Oh, Lord, this is painful and so limits what I can do," I complained.

In the silence a light dawned, spotlighting this object lesson for the conference.

"Thank you, Lord, that I hurt my arm. Thank you because it's a great way to put into practice what I'm going to say in my speech." At this, I laughed. Since my other speech was on the healing power of laughter, it was all coming together—the good medicine of Proverbs 17:22 and the remedy of thanksgiving in Ephesians 5:20. A perfect fit.

Until the next day when the phone rang at the yawn of dawn and a neighbor delivered good news, or what at the moment seemed good news. "We spotted your calf in the woods near our house."

Hubby hitched up the horse trailer and we headed out. Two miles away, we saw the steer grazing in thickets. Chasing him through brambles, down hills, and up bigger hills, I forgot about my aching arm. Finally, my husband roped him. There was pulling and lots of grunting. But the *steer* didn't make a sound—or move.

"Get behind him; grab his tail and twist it up. That'll get him going," my husband cheerily encouraged.

What was this? Some kind of pull-my-finger joke? I wasn't falling for it. Instead, when my husband pulled on the rope, it cut off the steer's wind, temporarily causing him to lose consciousness. As the poor beast crashed to the ground, he took me with him.

Boy, was my husband mad. What was I doing messing around back there? How were we going to get the bovine loaded with me pulling stunts like that?

Hauling myself up, I could tell things weren't right, but finished helping load the steer, rode home in agony, practically crawled into the house and collapsed on the couch. No going to work today. As mourning—oops, morning—turned to afternoon, my pain was so intense I could stand it no longer. It was all I could do to get to the phone to call for a doctor's appointment.

Once there, it was even harder to get from the car to the waiting room. My knee was swollen to the size of a cantaloupe. Finally in the doctor's office, I related my story. Perhaps I should have been a bit less humorous in the telling of it because Doc chortled at my tail tale, gave me, or I should say, sold me a pair of crutches, and sent me on my way without x-rays.

"If you're not better in a couple of weeks, come back," he said, revealing a row of white teeth.

Because my arm was still killing me, I couldn't use a crutch on my right side, so I bought a cane. (If you ever see a woman staggering about with a crutch under her left arm and a cane in her right hand, please have mercy and don't tell her she'd be better off using two crutches. She might hit you.)

Another object lesson? Maybe I didn't get the point the first time. "Okay, God. Thank you that I hurt my leg. And my ankle. And my kneecap."

Although I didn't think this whole mess was particularly funny, the absurdity of it made me laugh. Determined to apply the scriptural principles I would be touting, I continued, "Thank you because this makes for a great Show-and-Tell in my speech. Thank you that it continues to bring me back to you." By the time I had finished giving thanks, I can honestly say my focus was not on the incredible pain I'd felt moments ago.

Prepared spiritually, mentally, and emotionally, I was ready for the conference. Mexico was sunny and the heat immediately ministered to my aching body. My opening presentation on laughter garnered a standing ovation. These women were fun and embraced me with open arms. But would they be so welcoming the second day when I delivered a speech that most likely wouldn't fit into their beliefs? I continued to pray for them, and for me.

The next morning, I opened with the drama monologue God had given me in the middle of the night several weeks prior. As I delivered the play, I felt His hand on me and on others in the room. Afterwards, several came forward to share how they had been moved or had received insight by the presentation. While not everyone responded in like manner, I have prayed that God would water the seeds He planted that day.

Finished with my presentation, I could no longer physically stand. The plane trip home and traversing through the Los Angeles airport was a nightmare.

Following my return, and after x-rays, an MRI, and a bone scan, I learned I had fractured my foot, had stress fractures in my leg, and had broken both sides of the tibia just below the kneecap.

Upon hearing of the severity of my injury, my husband—bless his sweet and sensitive heart—went to an estate sale and bought a 1940-ish wheelchair.

"Thank you, God!"

When I told my husband he was in the book I was writing, he puffed out his chest and said, "Yeah, and they threw a planter in with the wheelchair, all for five bucks!"

What a guy.

Agony and physical therapy filled the following months. During the day I neglected drinking fluids to avoid trips to the restroom. Nights were worse. A comfortable position for my leg simply did not exist. Depression descended, dumping doubt of my ever being able to walk normally again. It was extremely difficult to thank God for the injuries. However, each and every time I did, it took my mind off the pain and the depression. It brought me closer to the Lord.

Although the process was grueling, challenging, and lengthy, thanking God revived my soul via seeing women blessed by my presentation. I gained wisdom from observing how God brought good out of my pain. I entered into the joy of being an instrument of His Word. It brought light to my eyes, having overcome the darkness of despair. It helped me endure through the pain. And it gave me great reward—I am equipped with more strength than before. Who but God knows if, like Joseph, my path will have made a difference in even one person's life—whether she is a woman from the Mexico conference or someone reading this book?

Praise His Holy Name! Psalm 19:7-11 indeed bears repeating ...

"The law of the LORD is perfect, reviving the soul. The statutes of the LORD are trustworthy, making wise the simple. The precepts of the LORD are right, giving joy to the heart. The commands of the LORD are radiant, giving light to the eyes. The fear of the LORD is pure, enduring forever. The ordinances of the LORD are sure and altogether righteous. They are more precious than gold, than much pure gold; they are sweeter than honey, than honey from the comb. By them is your servant warned; in keeping them there is great reward."

ᔪ

―――――――――――― ∽ ∾ ――――――――――――
☾ Invitation to Personal Reflection: Cause and Conclusion ☽

Looking back over difficult situations you have endured, can you now see why God allowed them to happen? Or perhaps what you gained as a result of a difficult time?

What did you learn? How are you stronger? How are you better prepared to weather the next storm?

The following space is devoted to your recording and to helping you see in your own handwriting the wonderful results of your trials.

Trial #1

_____

From this I learned:

_____

_____

_____

_____

Trial #2

_____

From this I gained:

_____

_____

_____

_____

Trial # 3

_____

Because of this, I am stronger in this way:

_____

_____

_____

_____

_____

Trial # 4

_____

As a result, I am better prepared for the next storm in that:

_____

_____

_____

_____

_____

━━━━━━━━━━━━━━━ ∽ ∾ ━━━━━━━━━━━━━━━

☾ Invitation to Personal Prayer ☽

Lord, in my spirit I want to be fully committed to you but in my flesh I often want what I want. Help me yield to my spirit's yearning ... that part of me that cries "Abba, Father," and that part of me that knows beyond comprehension that I can trust you with my life. Amen.

━━━━━━━━━━━━━━━ ∽ ∾ ━━━━━━━━━━━━━━━

☾ Memory Verse ☽

"For the eyes of the LORD range throughout the earth to strengthen those whose hearts are fully committed to him."
2 Chronicles 16:9

116

∿ 13 ∿

Where Am I in the *What Is?*

"Many are the plans in a man's heart, but it is the
LORD'S purpose that prevails."
Proverbs 19:21

"Should you shield the canyons from the windstorms,
you would never see the beauty of their carvings."
—Elisabeth Kübler-Ross

Being the compliant person I am—although my husband might say otherwise—
I agreed to speak on a subject about which I was less than enthused.

As a community college Counselor, I could cover subjects such as *The Healing Power of Laughter and Play, Bouncing Back from the Blues,* or *Fearlessly Fighting Fear.* But the conference planners wanted to know *Which Comes First, a Career or a Major?* First of all, there is no answer to that. Well, there is, but it's, "It depends."

Thanks a lot for not letting me pick my own topic, I grumbled, preparing for the dreaded challenge.

The day arrived; I was ready. At least I thought I was.

Although I was assured equipment and Internet access were up and running, I arrived early just to make sure. Sure enough, the laptop and projector weren't connecting.

117

Optimistically awaiting the technician I had called to fix problem number one, I circulated through the audience, acquainting myself with participants and their objectives in attending. To my chagrin ... no, it was stronger than that ... to my horror, I discovered instead of my promised target audience, in front of me were people who already had a career and/or major. They wanted me to find them a job. Problem number two.

Uuurrrch. My mental gears ground to a halt, shifted into reverse, and whirred, *How can I salvage this situation?*

Plan B. Scratch head. Gulp. Clear throat. *Plan B. The ol' make-it-up-as-I-go-and-see-where-I-get-to.*

Two technicians appeared. They got the PowerPoint operational and left.

Whew! I could take my eager out-of-work hopefuls to useful Internet sites.

Problem number one morphed into problem number three. Although the projector and laptop worked, I still couldn't access the Internet.

Re-enter technicians.

I'm dying up here. Stall. Pull a hat out of the rabbit. Engage participants in meaningful conversation. "Yes, um, I see you have your resume in hand." *Anyone here who doesn't? My husband is wrong ... there are times I am at a loss for words.*

With ten minutes left of my one-hour talk, my sought-after website finally appeared. *Big deal ... not enough time to resuscitate this casualty.*

"Okay, group. Thanks for coming. You've been great." Smiling, I internally sulked out of the room, huffed home and moped. I hated bombing on an assignment and had difficulty accepting defeat.

That night, I awoke at 2:30 a.m. and couldn't sleep. Tossing and turning mentally, I wrestled with the image of how badly the whole thing had gone. *If only I had .... I should have .... I could have ....* I simply couldn't come to terms with the situation.

Elisabeth Kübler-Ross's stages of grieving sprang to mind. I'd been stomping up and down these steps but now I could see more clearly the staircase: Denial. Anger. Bargaining. Depression. Acceptance.

Denial

Stuck in denial, I refused to believe the workshop was a dismal failure. I was freeze-framed in a picture of how I wanted things to be. Reality simply seemed not to be an actuality. I wanted to believe I came across as a professional, engaging in spite of the circumstances. There was no way I would accept that I conducted a useless seminar.

Anger

Angry I was unable to change things, I fumed over appearing unprepared and unprofessional. I felt powerless, helpless. The greater my feeling of power-lessness, the greater my degree of anger. *I confirmed the AV setup weeks ago*; I got mad at others for their part in all of this. I conjured up a case of revenge ... *See if I ever do a presentation for them again!*

Bargaining

Herein hovered my couldas and shouldas. *If only I could have chosen the workshop topic. I should have refused to accept this speaking engagement in the first place. Then this never would have happened.* No matter how many times I replayed these scenarios and rearranged my mental furniture, it still didn't change things.

Depression

There was no hope for things to be different. The fact was I failed to pro-vide workshop attendees useful information. Dark clouds of regret unleashed a torrent, dampening my spirit.

Acceptance

I didn't like what happened, but I recognized that it did. There was nothing I could do to change the situation, therefore I must move on.

∾

In reality, I didn't move through these stages quite so quickly. Nor did I do so by myself. My Divine Counselor led me along the path to Acceptance. As I lay staring into the darkness, both literally and figuratively, the Holy Spirit brought me once again to Ephesians 5:19-20. " ... *Sing and make music in your heart to the Lord, always giving thanks to God the Father for everything in the name of our Lord Jesus Christ.*"

Sing and make music? *Now, Lord? It's the middle of the night.*

Knowing the futility of resisting the exhortation, without further argument I obeyed. "Thank you, God, that my presentation was not as I'd planned. Thank you that it went awry from the start. Thank you that I came across as unprepared."

Within minutes, I no longer arm wrestled powerlessness. Instead of mental anguish, I moved away from a desire to be in control to a position of alignment with actuality. No longer caught up in the imagined control of *How Things Ought to Be*, I now rested in the *What Is*.

God resides in the *What Is*—a place of peace.

Thank you, God, for What Is.

Oh, and thank you that I didn't get to pick the topic for my presentation, for this whole thing brought me back to that perfect place in the What Is.

> *"I keep the telephone of my mind open to peace, harmony, health, love and abundance. Then, whenever doubts, anxiety, or fear try to call me, they keep getting a busy signal—and soon they'll forget my number."*
> —Edith Armstrong

It is impossible to run freely along our path when we are stuck in denial or anger—entrenched in wanting to be in control rather than accepting *what is*.

One of these days I'll get it right ... most likely later than sooner.

We will never be able to number the awesome things of our Lord, but one of the neatest things about Him is that He gives us so many chances to get it right. At this I am reminded of the four P's of getting it right. Practice. Practice. Practice. Practice. Even though I can't count God's amazing attributes, I can count on Him to provide me with always one more practice session. In my case, I am amazed at how He uses animals in the bargain, and has from the get-go. (In the Garden of Eden He used a serpent. Later, He used Balaam's donkey.) With me, He utilizes our cows. Maybe I should record these as parables, since they are indeed symbolic narratives the Lord employs to convey a truth or moral lesson.

I invite you to accompany me on yet another of God's provision for a *what-is* opportunity I had the not-so-much-pleasure of a while back.

Gone

Finally, Friday. I skim along Interstate 5 toward home, smug that I've tiptoed through this day without tripping over trouble. Last evening, when I unloaded my hellacious work week into the phone and onto my daughter, she said, "You still have a day to go."

High on disproving her foreshadowing, and hoisted by hope for a relaxing weekend, I approach our little ranch and skid to a halt—mechanically and mentally.

Now what?

Taped to the iron gate barricading our driveway, a paper flaps in the breeze, as if bent on breaking bad news.

Max and Frank hip and hop and bark and wag at my arrival. If they know what this is all about, they don't divulge much, the dirty dogs.

Why not just ignore the note? Part of me wants to, but curiosity cuts in.

I pluck the message from its position of adhesion, and read: "Are you missing a red cow? One showed up on our place today." The announcement includes a name and telephone number.

I push through a thick veil of denial and emerge on the other side into dread, which beckons me to take stock of all three pasture gates. Locked. Check. I walk the upper fence line. None down. Check. I check the barn—no cow.

Aaagghhh! *The beef's to be butchered in a week and I've already sold both halves. And collected deposits. I should've locked her in the barn.*

The other and most important reason this bovine can't be missing is that my husband, the one-and-only cattle wrestler on the premises, is elk hunting in Idaho—for another seven days.

Where is that man when I need him?

Once in the house, I dial the phone number. "Can I come see if this is my cow?"

"Sure." The lady does not sound as threatening as I imagined the note to be. Things are looking up.

I drive a mile down the road and wheel into the nice lady's place. Sure enough, my heifer stands chewing her cud, fenced in the front yard. What am I going to do? I have no way of getting Red home. Cattle are not like horses that can be led by a rope, at least not Red. I can't be so presumptuous as to ask this lady and her nice husband, who has now joined us, to keep my eight-hundred-pound animal for a whole week. And I would never be so outlandishly rude as to request that they allow the meat processors to kill her in front of their picture window. I don't know these people; I've never even seen them before.

What am I going to do? If I had locked Red in the barn I wouldn't be in this pickle.

"I'm in a pickle," I say. "My husband is hunting in Idaho. I have no way of getting the critter home. Would you mind keeping Red penned up until next Thursday?"

I can't believe my ears.

"And would it be okay for her to be slaughtered here?"

I don't believe my mouth.

The pleasant people say yes and hope it doesn't rain because if it does, Red's hooves will tear up their neat, grassy yard. I tell them I will come morning and evening to feed Red. The man says he will water her. Good, because I don't know how I will carry buckets of water in my car.

Wait a minute. How will I carry hay to her? In my two-year-old Camry, of course.

Okay, the lesson here is to trust that I can do all things through Christ who strengthens me. Still, where is my husband?

In Idaho, in his hay-hauling pickup.

But if I have learned anything until now it is to quit fiddlefogging around with the shouldas and wouldas and get down to business thanking God for this unique, wonderfully challenging situation. *Thank you, Lord, that Red got out and ended up in these nice people's yard. Thank you that they are willing to board her until Thursday. Thank you that not only is Red gone from our place, but that Bob is gone as well. For that prompts me to turn to you, to depend upon you, and to trust you with all of this.*

The thanks giving works in giving the boot to stress mounting in my body. I relax, at least for the moment.

The next morning I rise, not too bright, but early. I pull into the polite people's yard and pull out a big garbage bag stuffed with hay. These folks have dogs. Lots of dogs. Lots of barking dogs. I recall the nice man said he works a grave-yard shift. I wonder, at this moment, if he is asleep—or if not, if he is still as nice.

I talk myself through this. *I can't change the fact that Red made a break for it. I can only change my response to the situation. I can choose to be frantic, or I can try to see the humor in it.* Okay, so that's a stretch at this point; but I guess that's the point.

I do this three more times over the weekend and again before work on Monday. I am now out of hay and Red has munched every blade of grass in their yard. So, after work I stop by Westside Feed and back up to the loading dock where I hop out and make a request to a young man with bulging biceps. "I'd like a bale of hay, please." He looks at me, at my late-model auto, then back at me. I yank open the back door. "Thow 'er in there," I say.

Driving home I can hardly breathe. The bundle of dried, long-stemmed pasture grass wastes no time in making this small space its new barn, and sucks every bit of fresh air from the interior and out of my lungs. I consider opening windows, but the bound sprigs of stalks and seeds and stuff threaten to explode into a whirlwind around my head.

The next morning following Red's feeding routine, I emerge from my hay-hauler in the parking lot of Lower Columbia College where I am on the faculty. Immediately, my eyes fix upon substances sticking out of my Toyota's back door. Glancing nonchalantly over my shoulder to scan the area, I hasten away.

Tomorrow, I'll park down the block out of sight of my colleagues and students—who I teach about self esteem.

When I get to my office, I pluck sprigs of stems and seeds and stuff off my clothes and shake my hair out over the wastebasket.

Days blend into darkness. I lie awake at night and pray for no rain and pray for more help, because I don't know these people and how could I have asked them to do this? What if the butcher leaves a mess? How would my husband handle this? I must take the day off from work to be there.

I can do this. I can do all things through Christ who strengthens me.

I spend the week gathering a shovel, tarps and buckets, and tubs and paper towels, and lots and lots of apples to lure the cow onto the tarpaulin. I will instruct the man to shoot once I have her positioned. Already, guilt of leading Red to her death sucks me into a dark hole. Especially since I am fond of this sweet animal. She comes running whenever I have something in my hand. Red trusts me.

How did I get into this predicament?

Now I remember. It's because Red didn't breed after two attempts, and my husband—who is conveniently a state away—said she is only good for eating, and aren't I glad I won't have to feed her through the winter? The only thing I am glad about is that *I* won't be eating her.

Wherever my husband is, I hope he is having as much fun as I am. Thank you that Bob isn't here right now. (I am not thankful at all, but Ephesians 5:20 doesn't require me to be.)

Thank God He is with me, and every time I thank the Lord for this situation, stress slips away, and I rest once more in my Father's arms.

Thursday rolls in like thunder. The dread of the day wakes me, and I rise to travel the long mile to administer unsuspecting Red her last meal of hay.

I wonder if this falls under the "all things" category.

I pack the buckets, tubs, tarps, and shovel into my hay wagon.

Mustn't forget the apples.

The day slogs along—long, then longer.

At two-thirty the Death Truck pulls into my driveway. I lead it down the road. During this murderous march, my back seizes up. My mouth morphs into the Mojave Desert.

I find myself suddenly in the benevolent people's yard. Before I get out of the car, I take one last breath of hay, grab the fruit, and brace myself for what is to come. I will retrieve the tarps, buckets, and tubs from the trunk and spread them out, place the Winesaps, then go hide.

The Assassin has a much different plan. He springs from his Murder Mobile, a 22 rifle in his hand. "Is that her?" he asks, nodding in the right direction.

"Yes, but …."

He raises the gun to his shoulder, squints into the scope.

Wait!

Nothing comes out of my mouth. However, plenty flows from my eyes and from the depth of my soul. The grocery sack in my hand—which contains poor, defenseless Red's last meal and final pleasure in life, of which I deprived her—weighs me down.

Some time later, I collect my thoughts, along with stuff that used to inhabit my cow.

The kind man with the once-fine yard—before the week of Red and rain—says, "You don't have to clean this up."

But I do—have to. I make sure there are no remnants, and fill one trash bag after another with manure patties, and cart them to the trunk of my vehicle. They are heavy, but not nearly as heavy as my spirit. When that is done, I take up the task of filling a big tub with what was left behind by the butcher. The container is not large enough. I fill many more trash bags.

At last at home, arm weary with the smell of death on my hands, I sink into a hot bath of peppermint aroma therapy, guaranteed to relax and restore. I need to soothe my nerves and celebrate today—our thirty-seventh wedding anniversary. *Thank you, Lord, for getting me through this.*

Evening slips in, as does my husband. Without his elk.

"Happy Anniversary," he says.

At last, here is this man when I need him.

The next day he goes outside to walk the entire fence line. When he returns to the kitchen where I am fixing lunch, he slumps into a chair, takes off his cap, and hangs it on his kneecap. A sigh escapes his Idaho-parched lips. "I found where the heifer got out."

I stop stirring the pot of chili. "I checked everything up here," I say, certain I didn't miss anything.

My husband's eyes take on a haunted look. "Way down below. In the ravine. Elk tore up the barbed wire." He gazes out the window into the distance.

Thirty-seven years of marriage have prepared me to read his mind. *$500 for an out-of-state elk tag ... two days of driving ... when I could've ....*

Ah, yes, the ol' coulda, woulda, shouldas instead of meeting face to face *what is.*

I reflect on my week and am grateful that thanking God for each obstacle as it arose, helped me walk in the *what is.* Had I had to deal with Red's escape, relying on strangers, and dealing with the "Assassin" before I learned the value of Ephesians 5:20, I would have experienced unbearable stress and launched into a fit of anger at my husband for "putting me in this position." Praise the Lord that finally I got it right! Yay! And I know this will fortify me for any future *what is*—whether accidents, storms, or death that are part of life.

Thank you, Lord, for one more occasion to trust in you no matter what.

∽

Invitation to Personal Reflection

What coulda, woulda, shouldas do you cling to?

1. _____

2. _____

3. _____

4. _____

5. _____

What situations past or present do you mentally struggle to "control"?

1. _____

2. _____

3. _____

4. _____

5. _____

Invitation to Personal Prayer

Thank you, God, for What Is. And thank you for bringing me into accepting and residing in What Is. I place in your hands each of the above and ask that you help me truly relinquish control over them to you. Holding onto them has gained me nothing but misery and frustration. I want to accept what you do with them, no matter what. Amen.

Memory Verse

"And we know that in all things God works for the good of those who love him, who have been called according to his purpose."
Romans 8:28

~ 14 ~

In Which Camp of the *What Is* Do You Pitch Your Tent?

"But godliness with contentment is great gain."
I Timothy 6:6 (KJV)

Our dome tent perches on the south side of Mt. St. Helens at what feels like a 45° angle. We slide downhill, then scoot to reposition. Slip. Shuffle, claw back up. Repeat routine. We spend the night fighting gravity—and lack of sleep.

I paste this experience into my Enchanting-Adventures-with-Bob scrapbook. It sprawls next to the "Mary,-we're-going-across-the-mountains-to-a-desert-oasis" escapade already affixed in my mental album of unforgettable memories, where, even now, I am transported back to that particular time of premature visions when Bob made this announcement ....

In my mind's eye palm trees wave gently in a warm breeze, beckoning us to come hither, to kick off our sandals and refresh ourselves in the splendor of white sand and healing rays beside a pristine lake, which according to Bob, promises fish leaping for hooks sailing over the shimmering sea of blue-green water. With hopes of a relaxing weekend in a to-die-for setting, I eagerly spend hours packing and anticipating R & R, knowing for certain—than other than heaven—it couldn't get any better than this. The four-hour drive from home only serves to intensify this dream getaway.

Nearing our destination, I can't believe what I see. Abandoned appliances litter the landscape. Rusted-out car bodies, shells of their former selves, slump in ditches. Thistles and clumps of brown weeds nod in the wavery heat, proof of their prowess to replace palm trees. I roll down my window for oxygen and am punched in the face by a blast of an invisible inferno. I cannot breathe, but don't know whether it is from the heat or is a result of the sights sucking spit from my mouth.

"We're here," I vaguely hear my husband say.

In a daze, I follow him to the lake's edge. Ravenous mosquitoes descend upon us. Hours later, I come to my senses and find myself beside our tent pitched in a gully bracketed by two large lumps of dried mud alongside a river. Rocks the size of fists erupt beneath our sleeping bags and pummel us throughout the night. Coyotes slink about outside the tent, then throw a howling party. Just as the sun rises and we sink into slumber, a racket roars overhead. VAROOM. VAROOOOM. VAROOOOOOM. It sounds as if four-wheelers or monster trucks are racing up the dirt hills that embrace us, soaring from one mound to the other.

Bob peeks out the window screen. "They're not jumping over our tent," he reassures me. "Just whizzing around us."

These exploits represent only a couple of our family's tenting experiences that have set up camp in my head, lodged there like a fish bone in my throat. Lest I give the impression that all our excursions were miserable, I am happy and thankful to report many others proved to be pleasant and memorable. Somehow, though, they aren't quite as fun to tell.

෩

Just as we select a spot to erect an outdoor tent, so do we pick where we pitch our earthly tents, as Paul calls our bodies (2 Cor. 5:1). (Peter also refers to the "tent of his body." 2 Pet. 1:13) In short, it is our choice to spiritually, emotionally, and mentally reside in either Discon*tent*ment or Con*tent*ment.

Discontentment

Under the awning of discontent abound dissatisfaction, disgruntlement, discouragement, bitterness, resentment, blame, and hatred.

Although I am ashamed to share the following story, it exemplifies dissatisfaction and disgruntlement ...

On yet a different trip, while my husband drove north on Washington state's I-5, I was absorbed in my book, *Ordeal by Hunger: The Story of the Donner Party*. This plight of eighty-seven people, setting out from Illinois in 1846 by wagon train for California, captivated me. To make it over the Sierra Nevada Mountains before winter, they needed to chance a never-before-tried-by-wagons shortcut. Difficulties ensued, and by the time the party made it to the summit, they were caught in heavy snowfall. Trapped, they soon exhausted all their food. Deep snow prohibited hunting as well as foraging for anything edible. Makeshift shelters did little to keep out the cold. Starving and frozen, one by one they began to die. Eventually, the story goes, some resorted to cannibalism to stay alive.

I was at this point in history when my husband pulled into a gas station. "You have to use the Ladies?" he asked. I put down my book and headed for the restroom. Upon using the facilities, I rolled off some toilet paper. Disgusted at its coarseness, I mentally whined. *This is pitiful stuff. Can't they provide anything softer for customers?* For a moment more I continued to grumble. Then my thoughts jerked me up short. *At least you have toilet paper. Those poor people didn't have so much as a morsel to eat or a breath of warmth.*

The Donner party's members were victims of circumstances. I, on the other hand, was a victim of my own making with my "poor me" attitude. Feeling sorry for myself, I immediately assumed a position on the pity pot. (Sorry for the pun but the transition worked.)

Those who live in discontentment dwell in victim mentality. Discontenters' language is fraught with *Why me? Ain't it awful? You made me do it. You make me mad.* and *I have to* statements. *Have to* statements imply someone or something is making one do something. For example: "I have to do the laundry." "I have to take my mother grocery shopping." "I have to pay taxes." In essence, "Those people, those things are responsible for my burdens, my misery." This kind of thinking bans happiness from taking up residence in our lives, and in fact, bars it from even visiting.

In his book *thanks! How the new science of gratitude can make you happier*, Dr. Robert Emmons writes, "The tendency to blame others can be a strong resistance against gratitude. A sense of victimization leaves one wounded and mired in resentment and desires for retaliation ... when one's identity is wrapped up in the perception of victimhood, the capacity for gratitude shrinks" (137).

Following is a simple but practical technique to help you disconnect from this victim mentality:

Disengaging from Discontent Exercise

Write down three things you have to do today.

Example: I have to cook dinner.

1. _____

2. _____

3. _____

Now change these to:

Example: It is my choice to cook dinner because I highly regard my family's health.

Or: I choose to cook dinner because I want something tasty and nutritious to eat.

1. It is my choice to _____
   because I highly regard (or cherish) _____.

2. I choose to _____
   because I want _____.

3. It is my choice to _____
   because I place great value on _____.

When making these statements it is vital to phrase the second half of the sentence in the positive. For example, if you were to state: "It is my choice to clean the house because if I don't nobody else will.", then you stay stuck in victim mentality.

It takes practice to change your way of thinking, but the results are worth it. When you change your wording, you change your world to one of happiness. " … happiness can add as much as *nine* years to one's life expectancy."[5] I guess this is good news for both the content and discontenters, because why would the discontent *want* to suffer for nine additional years? But then again I may be wrong about that. Some people seem happiest when they are unhappy.

---

5 Emmons, Robert A., Ph.D., *thanks! How the new science of gratitude can make you happier* (New York: Houghton Mifflin Co., 2007), 13.

Now that you have the tool of changing "I have to ____" to "It is my choice to ____ because I want ____," you can easily cross the campground from discontentment to contentment.

When I reflect on my discontent over the rough toilet paper, I can't believe I grumbled over something so petty, and ask myself, "Why am I not always able to be content with what I have?" The good news for all of us is that the first step toward change is awareness. Once we acknowledge our discontent, we can step out of it and cross over onto the solid ground of contentment and gratitude. In addition to the "It is my choice to" tool, another simple way to make the shift is to say, "Thank you, God for what I have." In my situation it would have been, "Thank you, Lord, for this toilet paper." It's amazing how one sentence can humble a person and usher one's self into being content with reality—into contentment of the *what is*.

Contentment

Peace, hope, joy, love, self-respect, confidence in Christ, and knowledge of who we are in Him prevail in Contentment Camp. When we choose to be content and grateful for what we have—for it frequently involves a conscious decision—we sidestep stress and step into a state of well-being and happiness. In *thanks!*, Dr. Emmons, states, "Happiness is facilitated when we enjoy what we have been given, when we want what we have" (12).

Dr. Emmons goes on to say that people who experience gratitude feel more loving, forgiving, closer to God, and that they cope more effectively with daily stress, show increased resilience in trauma, and may recover more quickly from illness. His research reveals that "grateful people experience higher levels of positive emotions such as joy, enthusiasm, love, happiness, and optimism, and that the practice of gratitude as a discipline protects a person from destructive impulses of envy, resentment, greed, and bitterness" (11-12).

I read and hear of people who say they have trouble practicing gratitude daily, that sometimes they have to remind themselves to be thankful. The release for them from this obligation comes in Ephesians 5:20. What freedom there is in simply uttering thanks rather than having to be thankful.

One way to practice gratitude as an attitude is to keep a journal to maintain balance in your life. Some days you may have difficulty finding time to write or even list things for which you are thankful. Solve the dilemma by changing your routine to thanking God for situations as they occur. Upon the utterance of the words "Thank you, Lord for …," your mood is affected instantly and continues to be buoyed each time you give thanks.

Giving Thanks to God Acts as:

- A weapon against discontentment
- A shield against victim mentality
- A step toward fulfillment
- A calm after the storm of disgruntlement
- Rest for the weary of discontent
- A warm bath, washing away dissatisfaction
- A ray of sunshine, light piercing the darkness of displeasure
- A soaring wing, lifting us out of discontent's grasp
- Oil on discontent's parched skin
- Balm for a battered soul
- A refuge, a snuggle in contentment
- A currency of hope and purchaser of peace
- A gentle breeze, caressing us with joy in the *what is*
- A fragrant blossom unfolding a bud of satisfaction
- A pleasant spice of contentment
- An eagle's view of what lies below
- Wings helping us rise to remarkable heights

෨

Invitation to Personal Reflection

Listen to the words you use today, or this week. Record below the "have to" statements you hear yourself say.

_____

_____

_____

_____

_____

Now change them to show your choices and where you place importance in your life.

Ex: It is my choice to _____ because I highly regard (I want) _____.

_____

_____

_____

_____

_____

_____ ⁓ ⁓ _____

Invitation to Personal Prayer

Lord, thank you for showing me how I can move from discontentment to being content and from victim mentality to being more than a conqueror in Christ!

_____ ⁓ ⁓ _____

Memory Verse

"But if we have food and clothing, we will be content with that. People who want to get rich fall into temptation and a trap and into many foolish and harmful desires that plunge men into ruin and destruction."
I Timothy 6:8-9

∽ 15 ∽

Bountiful Harvest

" … For I know the plans I have for you," declares the
LORD, "plans to prosper you and not to harm you, plans to
give you hope and a future."
Jeremiah 29:11

Whose Plans?

Long awaited, I finally had a day off from work. At last, time for household chores clamoring for attention. But first I needed to take my car into town for service.

Up early, I drove the twenty-something minutes down Interstate 5 into Longview, Washington and arrived at the auto counter a few minutes early. My perfectly designed plans were off to a good start.

Our repairman scanned his appointment sheet, reading backward from the end of the day's log. His finger slid across two columns and up the page. Spotting my name in the 8:00 a.m. slot, he winced. "It's going to be quite a while before we get to your Camry. We still have several vehicles we didn't finish last night." He nodded his head toward the garage littered with cars, some on hoists, others with raised hoods.

I cringed and held my tongue, yet my mind rebelled against the unacceptable news. *An entire day in town without transportation and nothing close enough to take care of other business.* In a matter of moments, I reached a fuming pitch. I'd made this appointment three weeks ago for first thing in the morning so I could get in, get out, and get on with my day.

As I sighed in defiance, I heard my father's admonition, even though he is no longer with us. "Don't waste time." I hold tightly to this value and over the years have added to it—Make every minute count.

Rooted in the disgust of having to be stuck in wasted hours, with my feet planted in protest, I watched an elderly couple shuffle through the door and sidle up to the counter.

"We don't have an appointment, but we came in last night at closing and were told to come back first thing this morning." The man's voice dripped despair.

Just then a mechanic entered the lobby from an adjacent bay. "Yes, I remember you," he confirmed. "No problem ... I'll get right to your car."

Hey, wait a minute! Why you ... I have an appointment and they don't!

The Holy Spirit caught my attention ... and my tongue, before the words erupted from my mouth. In an instant, the Lord drew my eyes to what He saw—two people in their eighties holding hands, apparently stranded travelers. The husband seemed to be doing his best to encourage his distressed wife.

Feeling a bit foolish at my mental outburst, I silently prayed for them. Now in a better spiritual position to accept a long wait, I trekked the half-mile to the public library. My walk, showered by rays of sun, deposited me in the library's beautifully maintained grounds. Bracketed by old growth oak and maple trees on one side and a fragrant rose garden on the other, the park setting offered a shaded bench just for this moment.

The song, "In the Garden," hummed softly in my mind, followed by this message, *"You can spend a whole day doing nothing but praising and worshipping Me and you will have accomplished a great deal. Praise and worship glorify My name, rout the enemy, and bring peace to your soul."*

Suddenly, I realized that my earthly father's don't-waste-time admonition was no different from what my Heavenly Father now spoke. But for the first time I realized I didn't have to busily attend to a physical task. I relaxed and enjoyed the Lord's presence and all that surrounded me in the garden.

Encouragement from Psalm 46:10 to be still and know that He is God, helped me see the joy of being still before Him. Running in the path, while remaining still, was physically impossible, yet spiritually possible.

"Thank you, God, that your plans are not my plans. And thank you for the bountiful harvest we reap in thanking you for all things—miniscule or mighty."

THANKS GIVING HARVEST

Previously, I identified fruits we reap when we fear the Lord. Psalm 19:7-11 helps us recognize the bounty we receive when we keep God's commands: Soul Revival, Wisdom, Joy, Enlightenment, and Great Reward. In addition to these, following are a few other gains we reap from sowing seeds of thanksgiving.

- **Acceptance of God's Sovereignty**

Thanking God for everything brings us to a place of acknowledging and accepting that He is in control. This is not to say God *causes all* things, but certainly He *allows all* things. In her book, *when bad things happen*, Kay Arthur writes, "I also came to understand that the God who held me in His sovereign hand is a God of love (1 John 4:10). Everything that came into my life would have to be filtered through His fingers of love."[6]

We know He loves us, yet His promise that He has only good in store for us is sometimes hard to claim, especially when bad things happen. But just as in Joseph's case, what his brothers, Potiphar's wife, and others intended for evil, God—because He is sovereign—can bring about for good.

- **Position & Peace in the *What Is***

Acknowledging and accepting God's sovereignty however, does not automatically elevate us to that position of perfect peace found only in Christ. Still, acknowledging and accepting are vital steps into the peace of God which transcends all understanding. As we take those steps, the Lord generously offers object lessons which can move us into His peace.

If we prepare ourselves ahead of time, and in fact, establish a foundation of thinking that "what is, is" we shall be anchored in a seat of peace … that privileged passenger's seat beside our navigator, God the Almighty. Epictetus captured the essence of this position when he wrote, "When anything shall be

---

6   Arthur, Kay, *when bad things happen* (Colorado Springs: Waterbrook Press, 2002), 36.

reported to you which is of a nature to disturb, have this principle in readiness, that the news is about nothing which is within the power of your will."[7]

- **Prosperity**

Thanking God for unwelcome (in-the-grand-scheme-of-things), minor situations, as well as thanking Him for tragedies, allows us to accept that what has happened has happened, and there isn't anything we can do to change that. Wanting to change the incident or the outcome only sends us into a frenzy, causing us stress. Thanking God is about relinquishing control over external events. Since the only thing we have control over is our response to the catastrophe, when we "let go and let God," we experience inner release that moves us from victim to victor. It releases us from being taken hostage by the calamity. This is not to say we should avoid grieving. Sadness is a natural emotion, and we must not ignore it. But it is possible to be sad and give thanks at the same time.

In fact, giving thanks will help us be more emotionally healthy so we can grieve effectively. Unhealthy feelings that would ordinarily drain us of emotional health lose their power when we yield to God's commands. Fear falters. Anger abates. Resentment retreats. Anxiety vanishes. Of course, this isn't instantaneous. Just as when we are in the dark and light floods our face, it takes awhile for us to adjust our eyes. At first it is uncomfortable. But without the illumination of His commands, we are blind.

When our emotions are in a healthy state, we sleep better, experience better digestion, improve our chances of warding off illnesses. We are better able to focus on tasks at hand. Giving thanks releases us into healthy relationships, a positive outlook on life, hope for the future.

In addition to being more physically and emotionally healthy, our spirit also prospers. Allowing God's light to infiltrate every part of us helps us grow. By putting into practice Ephesians 5:20, we provide soil and water for God's Word to live and thrive in us. Our roots deepen; our foundation is strengthened. Our house is built upon our Rock. Rains may come and storms might pound, but we will stand.

John Newton, author of the song *Amazing Grace*, captured the essence of this when he wrote, "We will look back upon the experiences through which the Lord led us and be overwhelmed by adoration and love for Him! We will then

---

7 Long, George, translator, "The Discourses of Epictetus." *Great Books of the Western World* (Chicago: William Benton Publisher, 1952), 192.

see that what we once mistakenly called afflictions and misfortune were in reality blessings without which we would not have grown in faith."[8]

Thanking God for adversity makes us stronger for stronger storms ahead.

• Closeness to God

Suffering in and of itself does not necessarily lead us into a deeper relationship with God. It is only when we recognize the Lord's presence in our pain and when we reach out to Him, that we invite Him to take hold of our hand so that He might draw us close.

David wrote, "Though I walk in the midst of trouble, you preserve my life; you stretch out your hand against the anger of my foes, with your right hand you save me. The LORD will fulfill his purpose for me; your love, O LORD, endures forever ..." (Ps. 138:7-8)

One night I dreamed I was drowning. Torrents pulled me under; I spiraled toward death. When I cried out to the Lord, His hand came out of the heavens. As I thrust my hand upward, He drew me out of the deep waters and delivered me into a safe place.

Imagine my amazement, when later I read the eighteenth chapter of Psalms and saw my dream. My gaze was fixed on the verses as they unfolded the whole experience. When I arrived at the last half of verse nineteen, I was filled with awe. It revealed that the Lord had rescued me because He delighted in me!

This is the place I want to be—embraced in His love, in His grip of grace, and fully resting in His will. This is exactly where I am when I thank Him for all things.

In this most intimate of places, I get to know Jesus more and more. I increase in insight into God's character and will for my life.

• Maturity in Christ

It is vital for spiritual health to put our faith in The One Who promises—not the promise. When we focus on the promise, we may end up fixating on something we want to see, rather than what God intends in His promise.

Therefore, it is possible, when acting in obedience we may stumble into a snare. Whether a trap of the enemy or a result of our humanness, it doesn't matter. The pitfall is this: When we thank God for hardships, we may believe

---

8 Newton, John, *Out of the Depths* (Grand Rapids: Kregel, 2003), 12.

our obedience will bring a happy ending—consciously or unconsciously. In essence we are depending upon our actions for the outcomes we want, rather than depending on God and His will for our lives.

However, God's will is not subject to our expectations.

My sister in Christ, Betty, shared with me how she came to be in such a situation.

Betty's Story

At age thirty-eight, her husband faced open-heart surgery. Although Betty clung to God's promises of peace and comfort and His assurance that He would never leave her or forsake her, she vaulted over those vows to land on ground of her own mental making. She stood on the notion that her husband's heart surgery would bring about the salvation of her father-in-law. Her thoughts raced ahead to other family members who then would be saved as well.

Two days before surgery while blow-drying her hair, she remained confident of her conclusion and projections. Amidst the roar of hot wind, she heard a soft, familiar voice.

"What if your husband's father doesn't get saved?"

Betty countered, "What do you mean, Lord, what if? He *has* to." She stood, dumbfounded. "That's what this surgery is all about. If there is no purpose in this, I can't do it." She dropped to the floor, stabbed with the possibility of losing her husband—her lifelong friend—for no purpose. For the first time since the doctor's grim pronouncement, she felt alone, hopeless, and frightened.

In her desperation, scales fell from her spiritual eyes. Betty realized somewhere along the line her focus had shifted from God's sovereignty to her own will. Sobbing, she emptied of her emotions. A while later, ready to accept what the Lord had for her and her husband, she embraced His grace, knowing it was sufficient.

Today, Betty's husband is alive and well! Only God knows her father-in-law's future.

Disappointment and heartache await the what-ifs of our making. Thanking God without strings attached keeps us on solid spiritual ground. Surrendering to His will brings us sweet peace. Thanking God for His will keeps us from becoming self-sufficient in our own strength and belief that we have control. In this, we mature, becoming complete in Him.

- **Godly Understanding**

Do you still wonder, *How can I know God's will for me?*

Seeing things from God's perspective is a threshold to actually *understanding* His will for us. To understand means to grasp—to take hold of, to receive and make it our own much like when we accept a gift.

Understanding is one of God's gifts to us, one which He presents to us in the verses preceding Ephesians 5:20:

> "Be very careful, then, how you live—not as unwise but as wise, making the most of every opportunity, because the days are evil. Therefore do not be foolish, but understand what the Lord's will is. Do not get drunk on wine, which leads to debauchery. Instead, be filled with the Spirit. Speak to one another with psalms, hymns and spiritual songs. Sing and make music in your heart to the Lord, always giving thanks to God the Father for everything, in the name of our Lord Jesus Christ."
> —Ephesians 5:15-20

Here, God instructs that it is wise to use even evil inflicted upon us as opportunities. These words are "there for" us ("therefore") to grasp that His will is that we not turn to alcohol to drown our sorrows, or other things as many do, but to sing, make music in our hearts, always giving Him thanks for everything.

Understanding and dwelling in His will is a safe place to be. In fact in Proverbs 2, God promises that understanding will guard us if we accept His words and keep His commands.

What a mental image—Understanding standing sentry over us!

What protection, what security there is in that!

- **Godly Perspective**

One day as I was being all pitiful, feeling sorry for myself that God wasn't answering a particular prayer, I stood at my second-floor bedroom window watching clouds in the distance. The conversation went something like this:

"Lord, I've prayed and prayed. You tell us we have not because we ask not. Well, I've asked and asked. Nothing's happened."

"Do you see those clouds?"

"Yes."

"They don't appear to be moving, do they?"

"No."

"At least not from where you are standing."

"Right."

"From where I am, they are moving quickly. You see, I have much to put into place before the answer to your prayer comes about."

When God put it like that, I felt like a pathetic, whining child. When was I going to grow up, for crying out loud? Crying out loud is what I'd been doing, all right.

"What is the use of praying if at the very moment of prayer we have so little confidence in God that we are busy planning our own kind of answer to our prayer?"—*Thomas Merton*

Thankfully, putting Ephesians 5:20 into practice, has helped me move out of my own viewpoint and into God's perspective.

Death, abuse, and hardships of all kinds clarify things in a way nothing else does. When we thank God for these things, we put ourselves in a position of seeing them through His eyes. We realize what is really important. What is eternally important.

In his Psalms, David came to this conclusion when he wrote that it was good for him to be afflicted so that he might learn God's decrees.

As well, in his letter to the Philippians, Paul, (Leader of the Hardship Pack), wrote that he believed what had happened to him would turn out to be for his deliverance.

How could either David or Paul have written these things unless they had seen things from God's perspective? Since it was Paul who exhorted us to thank God for all things, I am convinced this is what brought him to a place of seeing things as God does.

C.H. Scott captured the essence of this principle in the first verse of the song, "Open My Eyes, That I May See":

> *Open my eyes, that I may see Glimpses of truth Thou hast for me;*
> *Place in my hands the wonderful key That shall unclasp, and set me free.*
> *Silently now I wait for Thee, Ready, my God, Thy will to see;*
> *Open my eyes, illumine me, Spirit divine.*[9]

Thanking God for all things, pushes us through the veil of human vision into His perspective. A wonderful example of seeing beyond our carnal scope is given in 2 Kings 6:17 wherein an enemy army surrounded Elisha's camp and Elisha's servant was freaking out: "And Elisha prayed, 'O LORD, open his eyes so he may see.' Then the LORD opened the servant's eyes, and he looked and saw the hills full of horses and chariots of fire all around Elisha."

This is a perfect picture of how it is when we believe we are outflanked by troubles. The reality is, because we are Children of God, we have a more powerful force surrounding us than that which we face!

- **Revised Focus**

In preparation for this manuscript, I approached several Christian women I knew to be dealing with difficult and heartbreaking circumstances. I disclosed that I was writing about the Biblical principle of thanking God for all things. Prayerfully, carefully in love, I asked if they would want to share their testimony as a vital part of the book.

I certainly understood when they declined. I was greatly saddened, however, by two responses in particular:

"I haven't gotten victory over my situation yet."

"I haven't come to terms with my child's affliction. I'm not ready to take the step of thanking God for it."

I, myself, have walked in this shadow of defeat. If only we all could grasp the illumination of God's commands, in instances such as these we would see more clearly. Stepping out in faith, doing what He asks, brings us further along the trail of understanding and victory. With His Word as a light unto our feet, we will not stumble in the darkness of difficulties.

When we fix our eyes on the problem and on our own strength and reasoning in trying to overcome, our efforts will never be enough.

---

9 Kingsbury, F.G., *Hymns of Praise* (Chicago: Hope Publishing Co., 1947), 377.

God does not ask or expect us to *be* thankful, but to trust Him enough to give thanks. When we do this, our gaze is redirected from our problems to Him. He is much more beautiful to behold.

The things of this world dim in the light of His Glory and Grace.

• Freedom to Forgive

Are you willing to apply God's thanks-giving precept in order to gain freedom?

I love Lewis Smedes' take on this. "When you release the wrongdoer from the wrong, you cut a malignant tumor out of your inner life. You set a prisoner free, but you discover that the real prisoner was yourself."[10]

When we harbor bitterness, resentment, or anger, we allow that thing, or person, to continue to harm us. Clinging to unforgiveness is like swallowing acid and expecting it to eat away at the offending individual.

> *"Anger makes you smaller, while forgiveness forces you to grown beyond what you were."*
> —*Chérie Carter-Smith*

Though strange and foreign to our human nature, giving thanks to God for abuse, violations, and other things we have suffered, is a step forward on the path of forgiveness. Healing lies directly ahead.

I have repeated it numerous times but again state: you don't have to *be* thankful. And again, God never asks or expects us to go to an abuser and offer him or her thanks for the harm done to us.

Forgiveness is not unconditional trust; so even though we forgive someone, it does not mean we would want to put ourselves one more time into the path of a perpetrator. Neither does forgiveness restore intimacy. When we forgive, we are not obliged to become emotionally vulnerable. Certainly, forgiveness is not an emotional state of warmth and affection. Nor is it a state of accepting responsibility for another's spiritual growth. As hard as it is to believe, forgiveness is not a disregard for justice.

---

10 Smedes, Lewis B., *Forgive & Forget* (Carmel: Guideposts., 1984), 133.

However, forgiveness is fruit of spiritual healing.

When we take God at His Word and thank Him for *everything*, we position ourselves in a place where forgiving others is possible.

In this, we become more than conquerors!

" … in *all* these things (trouble, hardship, persecution, famine, nakedness, danger, or sword) we are *more* than conquerors through him who loved us." (Rom. 8:37—italics and parentheses mine.)

Forgiveness is freedom. Freedom from the bondage of hatred, bitterness, anger, pain.

In short, we move from victim to victor.

• **Victory Over the Enemy**

Satan can't stand us giving thanks to God, especially if it is a circumstance orchestrated by the devil himself. (But allowed by God.) Even if Satan isn't the author of a tragedy, he finds ways to spring into the fray and tear our eyes away from Jesus. When we thank God for the adversity, we thwart the devil's plans to weaken or destroy our faith—or us.

Can you grasp the fact that thanking God is actually a weapon?

"The weapons we fight with are not the weapons of the world. On the contrary, they have divine power to demolish strongholds. We demolish arguments and every pretension that sets itself up against the knowledge of God, and we take captive every thought to make it obedient to Christ." (2 Cor. 10:4-5)

In thanksgiving, we corral our thoughts and obey His bidding. What wisdom and power there is in following His commands!

> *"Surely he will save you from the fowler's snare and from the deadly pestilence. He will cover you with his feathers, and under his wings you will find refuge; his faithfulness will be your shield and rampart."*
> —*Psalms 91:3-4*

Giving God thanks is not only a weapon but is armor as well, proffering protection from Satan's attacks! It is a shield of faith, deflecting the devil's lies—flaming arrows of the evil one, to coin Paul's phrase in Ephesians. Thanking God keeps those arrows from piercing us and drawing blood.

- ### Indwelling and Outpouring of God's Word

Absolutely every time I offer thanks to the Lord, especially when I am definitely not thankful for the situation, one or more Scripture verses immediately fill my thoughts. It is kind of like a boomerang effect. I cast words of thanks to God and they return to me with added words of His own … words of wisdom to wrap my mind and spirit around. Likewise externally, God's words wrap around me like a comforting quilt.

For example, on more than one occasion when the economy has taken a dive and I lose no small portion of my work retirement investment accounts, I have thanked God for these losses and He has returned my thanks with reminders that He clothes the lilies of the field without them having to work for their splendor and that if I seek Him first I will always have everything I need.

Memorizing Scripture is vital for spiritual health. When I can't quite put a finger on the actual address in the Bible, I am prompted to delve into God's Word to not only get the verse right but to see the context and grasp the bigger picture. The neat thing is that once I'm in His Word, it's easy to continue reading, thus I mine even more gold.

Also, in the instances when I thank the Lord for financial losses, He drenches the desert of my mind with the Jehovah-Jireh-my-provider song. What a refreshment! When I think of the future I rest in the assurance that *He* is my provider … not the stock market, nor my employer.

Other times, in other circumstances, my thanksgiving reaps the harvest of encouragement that I can do all things through Christ's strength (Phil. 4:13), that His grace is enough for me (2 Cor. 12:9), and that God has planned a wonderful future for me (Jer. 29:11).

I encourage you to memorize at least one verse a day. It will be like depositing in a savings account. The marvelous thing is that you can withdraw at any time but even better is that the withdrawal doesn't deplete the amount—it just keeps building with interest!

- ### Preventative Medicine

Just as a merry heart is good medicine (Prov. 17:22), so is giving thanks to God. And just as the Beatitudes are a prescription for preventing hardening of the attitudes, so is thanking our Lord and Savior for everything. When we give up trying to rationalize or justify why we shouldn't thank Him for the dark, the bad, and the tragic, we open our hearts to the care of the Great Physician. In other words, we move into prevention of hardening-of-the-heart.

"So I tell you this, and insist on it in the Lord, that you must no longer live as the Gentiles do in the futility of their thinking. They are darkened in their understanding and separated from the life of God because of the ignorance that is in them due to the hardening of their hearts."—Ephesians 4:17-18

Perhaps we could think of thanksgiving as a statin drug such as my spouse takes daily. For a bit of background … On the first day of the millennium my husband, Bob, died—twice. I must admit a certain amount of responsibility for his demise. When he'd complained of chest pains earlier in the day, I commiserated, saying, "Yeah, I know. I had that flu last week and it is brutal. Here, take one of my pain meds the doctor gave me last year after my surgery."

An hour or so later, Bob said his chest felt tight. "Yeah," I said, "my chest hurt, too. Here, take a little decongestant." When an hour later he asked me to call the health nurse and I did, she asked, "What color is your husband's face?"

"It looks a little gray."

"Call 911 immediately."

Long story short, Bob went into cardiac arrest in the ambulance and again in the emergency room. Praise God, they brought him back to life both times. Now he takes a statin drug to prevent his arteries from clogging.

Likewise, giving thanks allows the cleansing blood of Christ to flow through us. It prevents negative and harmful events from blocking our life pathways. When we offer thanks, bitterness is not given a chance to root, nor is resentment presented with an opportunity for residence in our hearts.

"Thank you, Jesus, for one more reason to thank you for your life-giving Word."

- **Blessings**

The Old Testament is laden with promises of blessings. Psalm 8:34 promises blessings to those who listen to the Lord. Psalm 29:18 and 119:2, and Deuteronomy 11:26 pledge blessings to those who keep God's law/statutes/commands. Revelation 1:3 assures blessings upon the one who reads God's Word and Revelation 22:7 guarantees blessings upon those who keep these words. These are only a few of our Lord's promises to bless us through His Word.

But what exactly are blessings? Are they tangible things like children, a job, a home? If so, then what if we have rebellious, meth-addicted children who have robbed us blind and pierce us with hurtful accusations? What if we are in a job so stressful we develop serious health issues? What if our house saps our bank account with mounting maintenance costs ... a leaky roof, rusty pipes, a clogged sewer line?

Or are blessings internal things such as peace, joy, salvation? If so, then would we want to believe that God has withdrawn His blessings of peace and joy when we're having a particularly bad day ... or life?

How about if we take the stance that blessings come in the mode of all the above? Even in the form of a leaky roof. Yep,

"For our light and momentary troubles are achieving for us an eternal glory that far outweighs them all."—2 Corinthians 4:17

this is definitely a thanksgiving opportunity and an opportunity for God to bless us in the bargain. With God, all troubles are opportunities.

When the steer fell on me, even though I endured excruciating pain and lengthy recuperation, and even though I tolerate discomfort years later, the blessing is that I am now on an exercise regimen, which as I age, will only serve to keep me mobile and head osteoporosis off at the pass. Another blessing is that I am more compassionate and sensitive to the needs of others in wheelchairs, on crutches, or those walking with a corrective boot. The looks of appreciation and thanks I receive when assisting or simply validating the person's pain and difficulty with a kind word of understanding are heartwarming—for both of us. It meant a lot to me when someone acknowledged and empathized with my agony and challenge, so I want to pass it on.

In similar but much more far-reaching fashion, author Ann Kiemel Anderson is an inspiration. Throughout her ordeal of miscarrying time and again, Ann stood firmly trusting that the Lord would turn her painful situation into something good. If you have read Ann's books or heard her speak, you will recall that she stands firm on the promise of Romans 8:28—meaning she can embrace her pain without resentment because she knows a blessing is on its way. Today, she continues to be in awe of the Lord's blessings—four boys she and her husband received through adoption.

Imagine the following in a cornucopia gracing your daily table. It may make thanking God for *all* things more palatable.

Summary of Harvest Reaped from Giving Thanks

- Acceptance of God's Sovereignty
- Position of Peace in the *What Is*
- Prosperity
- Closeness to God
- Maturity in Christ
- Godly Understanding
- Godly Perspective
- Revised Focus
- Freedom to Forgive
- Victory over the Enemy
- Indwelling & Outpouring of God's Word
- Preventative Medicine
- Blessings

༄

༄ ༄

Invitation to Personal Reflection

List your first ten blessings that come to mind. Do not take time to state them in order of value or meaning.

1. _____
2. _____
3. _____
4. _____
5. _____
6. _____
7. _____
8. _____
9. _____
10. _____

Ponder these blessings and record below which ones were borne of hardship or were what I call butterfly blessings—a gain from a loss. (A butterfly comes into existence only after the caterpillar dies.)

Your Butterfly Blessings: (May include the abstract ... insight, intimacy with God, joy ... as well as the concrete things in your life ... spouse, children, job, home, etc.)

_____

_____

_____

_____

_____

_____

_____

_____

_____

_____

_____

_____

_____

_____

୦ୁ ୧ୁ

☾ Invitation to Personal Prayer ☽

Thank you, Lord for the truth in Romans 8:28, that in my difficult situations, blessings are breezing my way.

Memory Verse

" . . . *but those who hope in the* LORD *will renew their strength. They will soar on wings like eagles; they will run and not grow weary, they will walk and not be faint.*"
Isaiah 40:31

(Did you know eagles wait for a gust of air to lift them up, and that they rely upon the wind to carry them without having to use their own power to fly?)

∽ 16 ∾

The Illuminated Life

"Your word is a lamp to my feet and a light for my path."
Psalm 119:105

Previous chapters have provided you occasion to give thanks for various things. Let us now see what an ongoing daily dose of thanks-giving might look like. See if you can identify situations you may have previously complained about. Turn the grumble into thanks and look for the positive in the situation. I hope this will escort you to a perspective different from one you previously had. May it lead to God's point of view.

Opportunities for Practice

"Thank you that my car broke down;
　　it causes me to see that I have a car to fix."

"Thank you, Lord, for the HUGE pile of laundry,
　　　　　　for that shows I've got puh-lenty of clothes."

153

"Thank you for my
tight
clothes,
because
that shows I have more
than enough to eat."

Thank you, Lord, that my sister is upset with me ...
This presses me to examine and understand my
behavior, motives, and my part in this situation. It also gives me an
opportunity to better understand her.

"Thank you for the
dirt ring around the
bathtub,
for that helps
me recognize and
appreciate indoor
plumbing and an
abundance of clean
water."

Thank you, Lord,
that I ran out of gas on
the Interstate. It reinforced
the fact that no matter what
or where, you are with me. It
also brought home the point
that situations like this are
not the end
of the world!

Lord,
I hate struggling with my anxiety disorder, but I'm going to take you at your word and thank you for it. I don't understand why I am afflicted with anxiety, but I trust that by giving you thanks for this condition, I will be able to shift my focus from the hold it has on me to the hold you have on me. The latter is much more comforting.

I give you thanks, God, for all this mud my kids tracked into the house. It compels me to remember I prayed for children and how wonderfully you answered that petition. It also draws my attention to how healthy and full of life they are. And, it points out that I am blessed to have a house and a floor to mop. It helps me keep my temper in check as I round up the kids to clean up. It helps me teach them the importance of cleanliness and being more thoughtful. It helps me role model loving discipline.

Thanks that my computer did "something" (it couldn't have been me, could it?) and lost my work of the past hour. This gives me an opportunity to redo my manuscript and make it even better.

Thank you, Lord, that this watermelon is mushy. It helps me appreciate the good ones that much more.

Let's take inventory of those things in your path, either ahead or behind you that need to be illuminated or eliminated ... those caverns of darkness, shadows of bitterness, pits of destruction, or boulders of obstruction.

Begin by making a written rather than a mental list. For this first list, it is better to start with minor things rather than ones which left your world shattered. Wade in shallow waters before diving into the deep end.

- **Small losses you have incurred:**

  _____

  _____

  _____

  _____

- **Frustrations you have endured:**

  _____

  _____

  _____

  _____

- **Physical aches you have suffered:**

  _____

  _____

  _____

  _____

- **Rejections** (not emotionally shattering ones just yet) **you have experienced:**

  _____

  _____

  _____

  _____

- **Betrayals or wrongs** (ones more aggravating than consuming) **others have done to you:**

_____

_____

_____

_____

Now, pick from your list and begin what may be a difficult step, but one which will stamp out roots of bitterness, resentment, pride or pain. Along this path, you will sow seeds of forgiveness and acceptance. You will reap a harvest of healing and freedom.

1. **Thank you, Lord,**

for _____

It causes me to see that

_____

_____

If you are having difficulty filling in the second half of the sentence, it may be because you aren't quite ready for that big of a leap. It's okay. Taking small steps is a beginning. You also may be thinking that filling in the last part is too much like "being" thankful for the situation, rather than simply "giving" thanks. If that is the case, leave these spaces blank until you can move on to the understanding part.

2. **Thank you, God, for**

_____

_____

It helps me to understand

_____

_____

3. **Thank you, Heavenly Father that**

_____

_____

This shows that

_____

_____

With these steps planted, you are now ready to advance to more difficult situations. Ones that will help you see how God has worked all things for good.

For example, "Thank you for allowing the beatings I endured as a child, for they helped me develop inner strength and drew me to you, Lord."

"Thank you for my unwanted divorce, for through it I discovered who I am in Christ."

"I give you thanks, Jesus, for the death of my child. Lord, this is the hardest one of all, and I'm acting out of obedience here, for you know I can never *be* thankful for this tragic loss. But, I will continue, trusting that when I take up your Command Illuminator, I will see a brighter path and gain great reward. Thank you for taking my sweet three-year-old son to be with you in heaven, for I can have assurance that all the days of his life are happy and blessed. Thank you for keeping him safe, for I also have assurance that one day we will be reunited! Losing my toddler has caused me to search you out, Lord, has challenged me to grow in my faith, and has helped me hide your Word in my heart. Today I am stronger, more resilient to daily annoyances. I have more compassion for others in grief. I have more appreciation for life, knowing it is death that gives meaning to life. I know the truth of Psalm 25:10—that for those who keep your commands, ALL your ways are loving and faithful. I know that to keep your commands is to have life, joy, peace, and great reward."

ᚦ

_____ ᚦᚦ _____

ᚦ   Invitation to Personal Reflection   ᚦ

_____

The following spaces are provided for your personal release of whatever God has laid on your heart to come to Him with right now.

_____
_____
_____
_____
_____
_____
_____
_____
_____
_____
_____
_____
_____
_____
_____
_____
_____
_____
_____
_____

൭

Invitation to Personal Prayer

Heavenly Father, thank you for leading me to this point of surrendering those things I have too long harbored in my heart. Thank you for taking them and working them for the good, for truly I do love you and take honor in the fact that I am called according to your purpose. As I reposition from the blur pain has caused in my spiritual vision, to your perspective, I know you are paving the way for my healing and freedom.

Memory Verse

"The LORD is my rock, my fortress and my deliverer; my God is my rock, in whom I take refuge. He is my shield and the horn of my salvation, my stronghold."
Psalm 18:2

~ 17 ~

The Sword of the Spirit

"Whatever you have learned or received or heard from me,
or seen in me—put it into practice. And the God of peace
will be with you."
Philippians 4:9

With the sword of the Spirit in your hand—the Word of God—you will walk and not stumble, run and not be afraid.

In thanking God for all things, we can do ALL things through Christ who strengthens us!

All is such a tiny word, yet infinite in meaning.

Perhaps the following path of Scripture verses—positioned together to present the complete message of *Run in the Path of Peace*—will help you put into perspective how this *all* works together to help us step into victory and be more than conquerors in our Christian walk.

In the following, imagine cobblestones forming a progressive pathway with each verse a stepping stone. (Psalms 19:7-11 is the threshold, with Romans 8:35-37 the end of the path.) Next, imagine yourself with your hands raised and your face shining. When you step onto the last verse, shout "I am more than a conqueror!"

Run in the Path of Peace Scripture Stepping Stones

Psalms
19:7-11

    Psalm
    119:165

        Psalm
        119:35

            Isaiah
            42:16

        Psalm
        119:105

    Proverbs
    3:5-6

Psalms
119:143-144

    Psalm
    119:71

        Psalm
        119:32

            Proverbs
            4:11-12

                Romans
                8:28

            James
            1:2-4

Romans
5:3-5

2 Corinthians
10:4-5

Philippians
4:12-13

Ephesians
5:19-20

1 Thessalonians
5:16-18

Philippians
4:4-7

2 Corinthians
7:4

Philippians
1:18-19

Colossians
1:9-12

2 Corinthians
1:3-4

Genesis
50:20

1 Peter
4:12-13

Philippians
4:9

Philippians
4:19

Jeremiah
29:11

Romans
8:35-37

NIV Bible Verses:

Psalms 19:7-11

The law of the LORD is perfect, reviving the soul. The statutes of the LORD are trustworthy, making wise the simple. The precepts of the LORD are right, giving joy to the heart. The commands of the LORD are radiant, giving light to the eyes. The fear of the LORD is pure, enduring forever. The ordinances of the LORD are sure and altogether righteous. They are more precious than gold, than much pure gold; they are sweeter than honey, than honey from the comb. By them is your servant warned; in keeping them there is great reward.

Psalm 119:165

Great peace have they who love your law, and nothing can make them stumble.

Psalm 119:35

Direct me in the path of your commands, for there I find delight.

Isaiah 42:16

I will lead the blind by ways they have not known, along unfamiliar paths I will guide them; I will turn the darkness into light before them and make the rough places smooth. These are the things I will do; I will not forsake them.

Psalm 119:105   Your word is a lamp to my feet and a light for my path.

Proverbs 3:5-6   Trust in the LORD with all your heart and lean not on your own understanding; in all your ways acknowledge him and he will make your paths straight.

Psalms 119:143-144 Trouble and distress have come upon me, but your commands are my delight. You statutes are forever right; give me understanding that I may live.

Psalm 119:71   It was good for me to be afflicted so that I might learn your decrees.

Psalm 119:32   I run in the path of your commands, for you have set my heart free.

Proverbs 4:11-12   I guide you in the way of wisdom and lead you along straight paths. When you walk, your steps will not be hampered; when you run, you will not stumble.

Romans 8:28   And we know that in all things God works for the good of those who love him, who have been called according to his purpose.

James 1:2-4   Consider it pure joy, my brothers, whenever you face trials of many kinds, because you know that the testing of your faith develops perseverance. Perseverance must finish its work so that you may be mature and complete, not lacking anything.

Romans 5:3-5   ... we also rejoice in our sufferings, because we know that suffering produces perseverance; perseverance, character; and character, hope.

2 Corinthians 10:4-5 The weapons we fight with are not the weapons of the world. On the contrary, they have divine power to

demolish strongholds. We demolish arguments and every pretension that sets itself up against the knowledge of God, and we take captive every thought to make it obedient to Christ.

Philippians 4:12-13   … I have learned the secret of being content in any and every situation, whether living in plenty or in want. I can do everything through him who gives me strength.

Ephesians 5:19-20   … Sing and make music in your heart to the Lord, always giving thanks to God the Father for everything, in the name of our Lord Jesus Christ.

1 Thessalonians
5:16-18   Be joyful always, pray continually; give thanks in all circumstances, for this is God's will for you in Christ Jesus.

Philippians 4:4-7   Rejoice in the Lord always. I will say it again: Rejoice! Let your gentleness be evident to all. The Lord is near. Do not be anxious about anything, but in everything, by prayer and petition, with thanksgiving, present your requests to God. And the peace of God, which transcends all understanding, will guard your hearts and your minds in Christ Jesus.

2 Corinthians 7:4   … I am greatly encouraged; in all our troubles my joy knows no bounds.

Philippians 1:18-19   … I will continue to rejoice for I know that through your prayers and the help given by the Spirit of Jesus Christ, what has happened to me will turn out for my deliverance.

Colossians 1:9-12   … we have not stopped praying for you and asking God to fill you with the knowledge of his will through all spiritual wisdom and understanding. And we pray this in order that you may live a life worthy of the Lord and may please him in every way: bearing fruit in every good work, growing in the knowledge of God, being strengthened with all power according to his glorious might so that you may have great endurance and patience, and joyfully giving thanks to the Father, who has qualified you to share in the inheritance of the saints in the kingdom of light.

2 Corinthians 1:3-4 Praise be to the God and Father of our Lord Jesus Christ, the Father of compassion and the God of all comfort, who comforts us in all our troubles, so that we can comfort those in any trouble with the comfort we ourselves have received from God.

Genesis 50:20 You intended to harm me, but God intended it for good to accomplish what is now being done, the saving of many lives.

1 Peter 4:12-13 ... do not be surprised at the painful trial you are suffering, as though something strange were happening to you. But rejoice that you participate in the sufferings of Christ, so that you may be overjoyed when his glory is revealed.

Philippians 4:9 Whatever you have learned or received or heard from me, or seen in me—put it into practice. And the God of peace will be with you.

Philippians 4:19 And my God will meet all your needs according to his glorious riches in Christ Jesus.

Jeremiah 29:11 "... For I know the plans I have for you," declares the LORD, "plans to prosper you and not to harm you, plans to give you hope and a future."

Romans 8:35-37   Who shall separate us from the love of Christ? Shall trouble or hardship or persecution or famine or nakedness or danger or sword? As it is written: "For your sake we face death all day long; we are considered as sheep to be slaughtered." No, in all these things we are more than conquerors through him who loved us.

Invitation to Personal Prayer

Thank you, Lord, for the illuminated path you have established for us so that we will not stumble as we tramp through troubles, and that we may have peace in the process. Thank you for showing us that the secret to contentment resides in thanking you for everything. And thank you that I can claim victory and am more than a conqueror! Amen.

Memory Verse

"I run in the path of your commands, for you have set my heart free."
Psalm 119:32

∽18∾

P.S.

"He will have no fear of bad news; his heart is steadfast,
trusting in the LORD."
Psalm 112:7

Remember when I wrote that after our fifth burglary there was nothing left to steal? I shouldn't have lied.

It was a cold day the end of January. January 24th to be exact. Arriving home from work, I drove into our driveway, got out of the car, and headed for the house. Just another ordinary day. As I stepped onto the porch, I noticed the door frame was badly damaged. Hmmm. My husband, presumably, had arrived home from work as well just minutes before. *He must have had trouble opening the door.* I entered the house, unalarmed.

Bob met me as I entered the kitchen. "We've been hit," he said.

Still nothing registered with me ... until I studied his face, which said it all. I felt sick to my stomach. Walking from room to room, I had great difficulty accepting the carnage my eyes took in. Drawers dumped out. Stuff strewn about. But the worst was yet to come. Our bedroom and computer room had been completely violated. The intruder had obviously spent at least a couple of hours going through financial records, our just-arrived order of blank checks, computer disks, and chests of drawers.

I don't have much jewelry, or should say, didn't have much jewelry; but what I did have carried sentimental value ... a twenty-four-inch gold chain with a locket on the end that my uncle brought back from Germany at the end of World War II ... real pearls my father had gotten in Japan when he served in the Navy in World War II ... my wedding band ... a college graduation ring my mother had had made for me using a diamond my other uncle's fiancée had returned to him ... a teardrop jade necklace my husband had given me.

On our twentieth wedding anniversary, Bob had presented me with this jewelry, which had two gold swans in the middle. When I opened it, he said, "You know when geese mate, they mate for life. Wherever the goose goes, the gander follows. I wish we were like that."

Talk about *The Language of Love!* (A book by Gary Smalley and Jack Trent demonstrating the power of word pictures.)

Now this was a period in my life when I was pretty much doing my own thing, most of which (women-type activities) didn't include my husband. That necklace changed my life. From that moment on, I went hunting with Bob, attended livestock sales, farm auctions, etc. And I actually enjoyed not only my time with him but the endeavors as well. That is, except for the cattle yards ode-de-manure, and the killing part of hunting.

All of that to say this ... what the burglar stole was priceless. And irritating. He didn't even go through my jewelry box, but instead dumped its entire contents into a bag or knapsack or whatever he used to cart off our belongings.

God, in His infinite wisdom, gently reminded me to thank Him for everything. And once again, without being thankful, I did. I would like to say my peace was instantaneous. But I'm sure not going to ever lie again! (That's probably a prevarication right there.) However, my peace did return eventually.

"Faith is belief and behavior walking hand in hand."
—*MaryEllen*

And I still carry the sentiment of each piece of jewelry. God nudges me to remember that my treasures are stored up with Him where thieves cannot break in and steal and where moths cannot destroy. Hallelujah!

There is much good to come out of this experience ... or the series of thefts. God is using me to minister to women who have had much stolen from them. Additionally, the Lord is using me to pray for each person who is now in the possession of one of my belongings. Although the burglary took place many months ago, when a particular necklace or ring, my laptop computer, or other missing articles come to mind, I lift up the new owner in prayer. Just as Paul prayed over aprons and handkerchiefs, I pray from a distance for each of these people to be drawn to our Lord and Savior Jesus Christ. What the enemy intended for evil, God will bring about for good. Hallelujah and Amen.

Invitation to Personal Prayer

Thank you, Lord, that you are using my losses for gains of souls into your Kingdom!

Memory Verse

"Do not let your hearts be troubled. Trust in God; trust also in me."
John 14:1

⌒ 19 ⌒

The Rest of the Story

"For in the day of trouble he will keep me safe in his dwelling; he will hide me in the shelter of his tabernacle and set me high upon a rock."
Psalm 27:5

Writing *Run in the Path of Peace* has been a journey for me. Thank you for staying with me to the end. And yet, this is just the beginning of the rest of our forever story in Christ Jesus.

Bless you for trusting the King of Kings and Lord of Lords, Creator of heaven and earth. May you heal from past and present pain and be free from all that has kept you in bondage as you give thanks for all things.

GIVE THANKS!

Gain
Incredible
Victory
Evermore!

Thanking
Him
Always
Nets
Kingly
Solace.

౸

"Great peace have they who love your law,

and nothing can make them stumble."

Psalm 119:105

౸

NOTES

Chapter I

Page

10   *King James Version:* Set forth in 1611 and translated out of the original Greek.

         Revised Standard Version: Translated from the 1611 *KJV*, revised 1881, 1901, and 1946.

11   *Phillips Modern English*: Translated from Greek Text, 1958.

         The New English Bible: Translated by a Joint Committee of The Baptist Union of Great Britain and Ireland, The Church of England, The Church of Scotland, The Congregational Union of England and Wales, The Council of Churches for Wales, The London Yearly Meeting of the Society of Friends, The Methodist Church of Great Britain, The Presbyterian Church of England, The United Council of Christian Churches and Religious Communions in Ireland, The British and Foreign Bible Society, and The National Bible Society of Scotland, 1961.

WORKS CITED

Arthur, Kay, *when bad things happen*. Colorado Springs, CO: Waterbrook Press, 2002.

Emmons, Robert A., Ph.D., *thanks! How the new science of gratitude can make you happier*. New York, N.Y.: Houghton Mifflin Co., 2007.

Epictetus: Discourses and Enchiridion. (Based on the Translation of Thomas Wentworth Higginson.) Roslyn, N.Y.: Walter J. Black, Inc., 1944.

Kingsbury, F.G. *Hymns of Praise Numbers One and Two Combined*. Chicago, IL: Hope Publishing Co., 1947.

Long, George, translator, "The Discourses of Epictetus." *Great Books of the Western World*. Hutchins, Robert Maynard, Editor in Chief. William Benton Publisher, Chicago, 1952.

Lucado, Max, *In The Grip of Grace*. Dallas, TX: Word Publishing, 1996.

New American Standard Bible. Nashville, Tennessee: Thomas Nelson Publishers, 1985.

New Living Translation. Carol Stream, Illinois: Tyndale House Publishers, Inc., 1996.

Newton, John, *Out of the Depths.* Revised for Today's Readers by Dennis R. Hillman. Grand Rapids: Kregel, 2003.

Smedes, Lewis B., *Forgive & Forget.* Carmel, NY: Guideposts, 1984.

Ten Boom, Corrie, *The Hiding Place.* New York, NY: Bantom Books, 1974.

The Holy Bible, Authorized King James Version. New York, New York: The World Publishing Company, 1913.

The Living Bible Paraphrased. Wheaton, Illinois: Tyndale House Publishers, 1971, 1973.

The New International Version Study Bible. Grand Rapids, Michigan: The Zondervan Corporation, 1985.

The New Testament in Four Versions. Christianity Today Edition. New York, NY: The Iversen-Ford Associates, 1963.

DISCUSSION GUIDE

Prologue:
1. Why do you think God honored the author's obedience in thanking Him for losing Tara to death, even when the author's attitude wasn't right?
2. In searching your Bible, which characters can you identify who railed against God?
3. What was God's response to them?

Chapter 1:
1. God led the author to present a message that initially she wasn't particularly thrilled about. Why does God direct us to do things out of our comfort zone?
2. What does God provide when He prompts us to do something?
3. What does 2 Corinthians 12:9 say about our weakness?

Chapter 2:
1. The author expresses gratitude for others' skepticism and questions when she shares Ephesians 5:20. Consequently, she has delved deeply into the Bible in an attempt to see this verse through God's perspective. How can anyone know what His perspective is?
2. At the end of the Q & A, the author presents an invitation to salvation, which breaks the flow of the discourse to this point. Why do you think she does so?
3. What doubts or questions do you have that the author doesn't address in relation to always thanking God for everything?

Chapter 3:

1. God told Noah to build an ark. Noah did, even though many believe it may have taken him somewhere in the neighborhood of 100 years! Then God told Noah to get in the ark with the animals. Noah did. He waited. And waited. Finally, it began to rain. How might Noah have felt shut up inside the ark for an entire week while nothing happened?

2. Why do you suppose God waited seven days before opening the heavens with water?

3. What other Bible characters waited a long time to receive God's promises?

4. Why do you think God doesn't always immediately deliver what He has promised?

5. What might it have been like to be the wife of Noah, Abraham, or Moses, and what character traits must they have needed for a successful marriage?

Chapter 4:

1. The Bible refers to God's commands, laws, precepts, statutes, and ordinances. What is the definition of each?

2. How are the above different—or the same?

3. What are some fences God constructs to keep us safe?

4. A sidebar includes Norman Vincent Peale's quote, "Change your thoughts and you change your world." How does this work?

5. How might changing one of your thoughts change your world?

Chapter 5:

1. In what ways do you see God's faithfulness to Claire, in spite of her sin?

2. How does this compare with God's relationship with King David and his sins?

3. What does 2 Timothy 2:11-13 say about God's faithfulness to us?

4. Discuss ways God sends us warnings to avoid sin.

5. Which of his hardships does Paul mention in 2 Corinthians 11:23-29?

Chapter 6:

1. In a sidebar, the author mentions the spiritual weapon of giving thanks. What are other spiritual weapons?

2. How would you differentiate between having joy and being joyful? Give examples of each.

3. Paul gives clear-cut ways to counteract anxiety, such as thinking about whatever is true, noble, right, pure, lovely, admirable, excellent, and praiseworthy. What other harmful or unproductive frames of mind might this mental exercise kick to the curb?

Chapter 7:

1. It is beyond our comprehension why God doesn't stop child abuse. Still, we know that what the enemy or others intend for evil, God can bring about for good. (Genesis 50:20) What good comes about for Marcy?

2. How would you account for the fact that some abused children turn to God while others reject Him?

3. Following Marcy's story, the author writes about the will of God. How does this discourse tie in with the chapter's theme "Light Pierces Our Darkness"?

4. Using your Concordance, select two Scripture passages that include reference to "light". Share these with your group and discuss.

Chapter 8:

1. How does each type of fear protect us?

2. Is it possible to experience both fears simultaneously? If so, when? If not, in what situations is it not possible?

3. When can peace and fear co-exist within one's self?

4. Jonah believed he was justified in attitude and behavior when God sent him to Nineveh. History shows the futility of arguing with God, yet we still do. What erroneous beliefs contribute to our hope that we will get our way if we persist in resisting God's commands?

Chapter 9:

1. The author describes her fear of an intruder in the middle of the night. What contributed to this being a rational fear? What did she do to escalate this fear to the irrational?

2. Psychologists maintain that we embrace thoughts and behaviors— whether positive or negative—because of a payoff, conscious or

subconscious. What might the author have hoped to gain from her wild imaginings?

3. What would she have gained from applying Paul's principles of substituting this type of thinking with the *Whatsoever List* (from Chapter 6)?

4. Paul encourages us to "not be anxious about anything." What keeps us from immersing ourselves into the *Whatsoever List*, therefore avoiding anxiety and full-blown fear?

5. The author mentions a spirit of fear sent from the enemy. How does Satan use one of his demons to drive us away from peace?

Chapter 10:

1. Paddy has no assurance that she will ever again have the relationship she and her husband previously shared. Her response is to make the most of what they presently have. What does one need to let go of to get to this positive place?

2. For many years King Asa relied solely on God, during which time he reigned successfully. What could have contributed to his falling away from trusting in the Lord?

3. What signs alert us to the decline of our dependence upon God?

4. What are your thoughts of the three promises in John 16:33?

Chapter 11:

1. The author presents ten must-do's when bad things happen. How have our busy lives nudged aside these simple, healthy activities?

2. What in our daily routines could we replace with these must-do's—all or at least some from the list?

3. Bring a CD and player to group to share your favorite praise or worship song. After playing, discuss the effects of the music and its message on each individual's state of mind, emotions, and spiritual wellbeing.

Chapter 12:

1. If you haven't read *The Hiding Place* by Corrie ten Boom, you may want to do so. Along with countless others, Corrie suffered at the hands of Nazis in Hitler's concentration camps. Some survivors have said God abandoned them there. Corrie contended until the end of her life that God was with her throughout the horrific experience. Why do you

suppose some feel abandoned by God while others don't, even when they share the same circumstances?

2. Throughout *Run in the Path of Peace*, the author repeats certain Scriptures, such as Ephesians 5:20, Psalms 19:7-11, and Romans 8:28. What is the importance of weaving these particular verses again and again into the fabric of the book?

3. What is your answer to the chapter's title, "Without Pain Where Would We Be?"?

Chapter 13:

1. Elisabeth Kübler-Ross pioneered the study of death and dying. If you were not previously aware of the stages of grief she identified, what insight did you gain from this portion of the chapter?

2. If you were already familiar with these stages of grief, had you thought of applying them to circumstances other than death? If so, in what situations?

3. Discuss losses where these stages could be applied, and how the process could be beneficial.

4. The author relates another bovine story and attempts to stir a sprinkle of humor into the pot of the pickle she is in. Discuss the benefits of laughing in the face of misery.

Chapter 14:

1. Why do we refuse to accept that it is our choice to wallow in misery?

2. Why do some people view circumstances as the determining factor for their state of mind?

3. The "have to vs. choose to" exercise is an empowering, freeing tool. What would we hope to sustain or gain by refusing to utilize it?

4. The author identifies several descriptions of what giving thanks to God acts as. (A weapon against discontentment, a pleasant spice of contentment, an eagle's view of what lies below, etc.) What images/metaphors/similes would you like to add?

Chapter 15:

1. The author states that when we give thanks, bitterness is not given a chance to take root within us. If you are a visual person and could

put form and a face to bitterness and resentment, what would each look like? Describe these in detail and as graphically possible—in living color—to your group.

2. Try to visualize these creatures thriving inside you. Discuss what might happen to your body, soul, and spirit as they continue to grow.

3. Freedom to forgive is one crop we cash in on when we thank God. Imagine what your body, soul, and spirit would be like if not even a trace of unforgiveness resided within you. Share this image with the group.

4. The chapter concludes with a summary of the harvest we reap from giving thanks. Which of these are now blessing you and producing fruit in your life?

Chapter 16:

1. During a routine day, how many irritating and/or annoying opportunities would you guess there are for giving thanks? Before your day begins, write down that number. As the day progresses, keep a tally of the incidents as they occur.

2. At the end of the day, compare the number you guessed to the actual count.

3. As a result of this activity, discuss in your group:
   a. I was surprised at …
   b. This exercise confirmed …
   c. I learned …
   d. From now on I intend to …

Chapter 17:

1. Share with your group your favorite verse from this chapter.
2. Discuss how it has ministered and/or empowered you.

Chapter 18:

1. The author states that much good comes from the thefts she and her husband have experienced. Write down those things that have been stolen from you. (Do not write your name on the sheet.) Fold and drop each member's piece of paper into a container passed around the group. After all are collected, join in prayer, lifting the perpetrator of each

stolen item to the Lord. It is important that you don't call out names, or even identify what has been stolen. Consider offering this prayer aloud: *"Lord, you are aware of each item represented here, and its thief. We lift each of these individuals to you for deliverance from the need to take that which doesn't belong to him or her. We also ask you to bless each of these persons with your love. Lead them to you, Lord, that they might know you as their personal Savior. We agree in Jesus' name to let go of the item that was once ours and ask that you bless its new owner with every spiritual blessing from above. Amen."*

Chapter 19:

1. In what ways does the GIVE THANKS acrostic embrace and reflect the message of *Run in the Path of Peace*?
2. Create a different acrostic for GIVE THANKS. If you have difficulty coming up with one, group think is a great way to brainstorm.
3. If you would like to share your acrostic or the one(s) your group creates with the author, she would love to hear from you. (See the email address on the back cover.)

COMING NEXT!

In the "I" of the Storm
Stories of Thanks-Giving

In the "I" of the Storm—Stories of Thanks-Giving will be a collection of readers' true accounts which demonstrate the power of thanking God for all things—the annoying, the awesome, and the awful.

If you are interested in submitting your story for consideration and would like to receive submission guidelines, contact MaryEllen at:
maryellenstone@hotmail.com
In the email subject bar type: Storm Submission Guidelines

If you would like to place your name and email address on the mailing list for notification of the release of *In the "I" of the Storm—Stories of Thanks-Giving*, email MaryEllen at: maryellenstone@hotmail.com
In the email subject bar type: Storm Address List

Submissions will be received until the book's quota is filled.

Made in the USA
Charleston, SC
08 January 2012